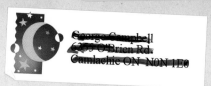

Journey to a Lonely Land

Journey to a Lonely Land

The Birth and Growth of the
Northern Canada Evangelical Mission

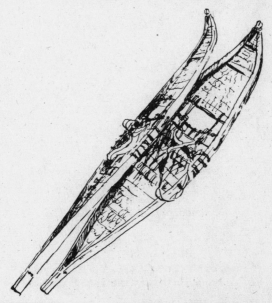

by Bernard Palmer

"Let us journey to a lonely land I know."

From "Call of the Wild"
by Robert W. Service
in **Songs of a Sourdough.**

Produced by
BUENA BOOK SERVICES
Box 600, Beaverlodge, Alberta, Canada
Printed in the United States of America

Foreword

Mention the northern half of Canada and most people think of a vast waste of lakes and forests and deep winter snows. A land where moose and caribou and ptarmigan abound. A land that man avoids.

A land of moose . . .

That picture is only partially correct. In many ways northern Canada is harsh and unfriendly. Roads creep slowly into the rocky, unsettled areas at great expense. In many cases only huge deposits of scarce minerals will make the cost feasible. But there are people there. And not just a scattering of prospectors and trappers living alone. There are isolated settlements all across the North, some with several hundreds of Indians. They fish and hunt and trap much as their fathers and their fathers' fathers did.

They speak a little English and increasing numbers are learning to read and write, but in the home they speak Ojibway, Cree, Chipewyan, or any of the forty-nine other languages. There are fifty-two tribes in Canada, each with different characteristics, personality traits and languages or dialects. And only a handful have a written language. Even less have the Word of God translated so they can read it in their mother tongue.

The white man brought them the gospel more than a hundred years ago and in some cases far sighted missionaries reduced tribal languages to writing and taught the people to read. (The most notable is probably James Evans who produced the Cree Bible in syllabics.) But the white man also brought the Indian his liquor, his dishonesty and his diseases. Most white men have long since forgotten the Indians. For many years while missionaries were being sent to the far reaches of the globe, Christians neglected the tribes to the North. Today only a pitifully small percentage have ever had the opportunity to hear the gospel of the Lord Jesus Christ.

Preparation for work in the North is much like that for most foreign lands. The would-be missionary must be willing to live in isolation and loneliness with few of the conveniences that are so much a part of modern life. He has to be prepared to live in a different culture than his own with different standards and values. He may be called upon to undergo ridicule and scorn, and must be prepared to work for years if necessary without visible results. Although English is spreading in the North, the chances are that he will be called upon to learn a difficult language.

The missionaries who serve in the North are a peculiar breed of men. There must be steel in the very fibre of their beings, a willingness to undergo physical hardship and discomfort. Not heroes, they. They would laugh to scorn the man who tried to place such a label upon them. But there is a toughness of character about those who succeed, a dedication of purpose that does not yield to defeat. The faint of heart may come, but it isn't long until they turn and steal away.

It is about such men that this book is written, with the prayer that it might make the reader aware of the needs in the North, and might be a challenge to Christian youth who sadly think the last frontier has been conquered. It is our hope that we can cause some to look northward beyond the farms and roads and modern cities to the land of the power toboggan, the traps and snares, the nylon fishing nets and the hunting rifles. We hope to challenge some with the needs of the North where many are dying every year without having the opportunity to know that Christ died for them.

This is the account of the NORTHERN CANADA EVAN-GELICAL MISSION and is limited to their missionaries and fields. Yet theirs is only one group among a number of faith and denominational missions dedicated to the salvation of our Indian brothers. This, then, is actually the story of all who serve God in the North.

The Author

Author's Note

This book is not intended to be an exhaustive history of the work of the Northern Canada Evangelical Mission. Only God could record all that has been done by missionaries and friends of the work in the past 25 years. No attempt has been made to search out the most effective servants of the Lord and reveal their activities as more worthy than those who go with little or no mention.

In some cases certain missionaries are included because of the author's desire to achieve what he felt was balance in the story. In others lack of space or information made it necessary to cut or eliminate the work of some of the most worthy workers.

Neither are the events set down in chronological order in every case.

The purpose of this book is not to glorify anyone except the Lord Jesus Christ. It is not even a complete history in the accepted meaning of the term. Rather, it is an honest effort on the part of the author and everyone else involved to inform and challenge Christians with the needs of our lost brothers in the North. If we can succeed in gaining a few prayer warriors for our Canadian Indians we will count the effort a victory.

Bernard Palmer

Contents

Chapter 1

"He speaks English — you teach him."

The chill sub-arctic wind ripped through the stark poplar forest from out of the north. Naked branches rattled noisily, one against the other, and long tendrils of fine, new snow whipped in ever-changing patterns across the storm-hardened drifts and rough lake ice.

The ski-shod Norseman had just landed on Lake Windigo in roadless northern Ontario. The pilot, engine idling against the cold, looked up at the somber slate sky, thinking again of the weatherman's ominous prediction. The last box of fish was put aboard and he was about to get in himself when a slender, dark-faced lad approached the aircraft, a cardboard suitcase in his hand.

"Stopping at Round Lake on the way out?"

The pilot nodded. "That's what I've been figuring, but I don't know whether I can take you, Albert. Did the boss say you could go?"

"You can ask him if you want to. He just paid me off."

The first time nineteen year old Albert Tait went to his employer and told him that he wanted to quit he refused to listen.

"You're too good a man to let go, Albert."

The shy young Saulteaux had tried to protest, but he could not grasp the words to express the longing in his heart.

The next time the plane came in he tried again to get this man who had hired him to help lift the nets and pack the frozen fish to understand that he had to go.

"But, Albert, you can't get a job anywhere this time of year

1

and I can't get a man to take your place. I'm paying you as much
as anyone else would give you. Forget this nonsense about quitting
and go back to work."

The youthful Indian stood mutely before him. Albert wondered
how he could explain that he was trying to run from the fierce
desire for alcohol that was beginning to consume him. How could
he tell another of the burning in his heart to get to Round Lake?
His boss would laugh if he told him he wanted to go there because
he had heard that a white man who could tell him about God lived
at Round Lake now. And, somehow, he had the feeling that God
could quench his thirst for alcohol.

The ski-shod Norseman had just landed.

Even before Albert went north to fish he loathed the liquor
he could not keep from drinking. Indeed, he had taken the job on
the isolated lake in the first place thinking it would be a place where
he could escape the bottle. But he had reckoned without the thirst of
his fellow fishermen or the frequent trips of the fish plane which
so obligingly kept them well supplied with liquor.

Albert's dread of Saturday night with its stupefying drunkenness
increased, as did his hatred of Sunday with its inevitable hangover
and gnawing disgust at himself for not being able to control his
drinking.

In desperation he turned to the Bible a cabin mate had brought
with him. He tried to read it but the sentences were long and the
words were hard to understand. He would have quit reading but
the thought persisted that the Bible had the answer to his problem,
if he could only find it.

One afternoon Alex came in and caught him reading it.

"I've been reading your Bible," he admitted, "but I don't understand much of it."

Alex sat down. "I saw a fellow from Round Lake a couple of weeks ago who says there's a white man living there now who's telling people about God."

Albert acted as though he had not heard. Actually, the words scarcely registered. But in the quiet of the long night he got to thinking about it. A man who was able to tell people about God ought to know what was in the Bible. He might be able to help.

The weeks went by. Albert continued to drink on Saturday nights only to resolve when he sobered up that he was never going to drink again. And he continued to talk to his employer about quitting his job and leaving. At first his boss ignored his restlessness or tried to talk him out of it. At last Albert was insistent.

"Please let me leave," he said. "I can't stay on this job any more."

"Albert, I need you and you need the work." Irritation tinged the white man's voice. "Isn't that enough?"

The young Indian's lips quivered. He tried to speak but the words would not come. Tears slipped from beneath his eyelids and trickled down his cheeks.

"All right," his employer said, softening, "if it means so much to you, come on and get your time."

And so Albert Tait, admitted alcoholic, crawled into the waiting fish plane and fastened his seat belt for the short flight to Round Lake.

*   *   *

Those who had known the handsome young Indian when he was a boy living with his older brother on the newly opened gold fields of northern Ontario, would have sworn that he would never amount to anything. He refused to stay in school and wouldn't study while he was there.

On one escapade when he was seven he attempted to hitch a ride on a huge truck rumbling to the smelter with a load of ore. His sweating young hands slipped and he fell beneath the rear wheels breaking both legs.

That meant a trip to Kenora and an extensive stay in the hospital. It also meant that the authorities became aware of him and clapped him in a boarding school.

He found them to be more vigilant and persistent than his brother who didn't care much what he did. If he ran away the authorities caught him and brought him back. After three years of formal education, however, he was through and no amount of discipline could keep him in school.

It was not easy for a boy to keep himself in clothes and food and get a place to stay, but Albert Tait was skilled at living by his wits. For awhile he worked as a shoeshine boy around one of the Kenora hotels. Later he had the same job at a smaller, more remote Ontario community.

Living as he did, it was to be expected that sin would soon grab him. He was drunk for the first time when he was fourteen and by the time he was seventeen liquor held him remorselessly in its burning fingers. In a desperate effort to free himself he left the town where he had been working and went north to help a commercial fisherman.

Liquor was not Albert's only problem. A medicine man told him that he did not have long to live. And a relative who dabbled with the spirits told him he could help keep him alive for two or three years, but that was all. He wasn't very powerful.

Albert, who believed that he could go to heaven only if his good deeds over-balanced the bad, was desperate to stop drinking. Now, at Christmas time in 1952 he was on his way to Round Lake, still fighting alcoholism. This time it was with the vague, desperate hope that perhaps the God of the Bible could do for him what he could not do for himself.

When the plane landed at the settlement Albert's cousin, was the first to greet him.

"I heard there was someone here who came to tell us about God."

"It is true," his cousin Isaac said gravely. "I've given up my drinking and gambling and sin. I'm a Christian now."

He could also have added that he was the only Christian in the settlement, and the first convert of missionary Cliff McComb who had come to Round Lake with his family a few months earlier.

Albert's face was devoid of expression, but there was an eagerness is his heart that set him to trembling.

"I'm alone, Albert," Isaac said. "And I've got two beds. Come home with me."

In the little log cabin the two men built up the fire and, sitting down together, began to ponder over the Word of God.

Albert was one who could not believe easily. There were questions that had to be answered first, questions that had plagued him since he started reading the Bible back at Windigo. For the first time those questions found voice.

"Why would God want to bother with someone like me? How could I do enough for Him to make me good enough so He would want to save me? How can God forgive the things I've done? How can God help me to quit drinking when I can't do it myself?"

Hazily, Isaac recalled that McComb had answered a number of those same questions for him. He didn't remember exactly what the missionary had said, but he knew that he had been satisfied with those answers.

"Why?" Albert persisted. "Why? *Why?*"

And Isaac could only fumble for words and shake his head.

For the next few days the two young men went over the Scriptures reading, re-reading, questioning——trying desperately to understand. But always there were the questions. Isaac was able to answer them partially, but not well enough to satisfy Albert.

"I cannot understand," Albert acknowledged slowly, as though there was sin involved in his very inability to grasp the meaning of what he read and what his cousin tried to tell him. "I try, but there are so many things I cannot figure out."

At that moment it seemed that his drinking and the burdens of his wicked life were heavier upon him than they had ever been.

"I think it is better for me to take you to McComb," his cousin finally admitted. "He can make the words as plain for you as he did for me."

After supper that evening the two of them appeared at the missionary's door. They had scarcely been ushered inside and the door closed behind them when Isaac spoke up.

"He speaks English," he blurted. "You teach him."

McComb had Albert and his cousin sit down and, starting at the beginning, he explained the way of salvation with painstaking care. But there was no indication of interest through the opaque curtain of Albert's eyes, no sign that the visit had not been at Isaac's insistence and his cousin was too polite to refuse. He asked no questions and made no comment. It had been a one-sided conversation from the start. McComb had a short prayer before they left.

"That's something I always like to do when my friends leave," he told Isaac and Albert.

But again there was no evidence as to Albert's reaction.

"Take this tract with you," the missionary said as they lingered for a moment at the door. "It explains everything I've been trying to tell you."

Without a word the young Indian glanced at it and stuffed it into his pocket.

When they were gone Mrs. McComb asked her husband, "Do you think you got anywhere with him, Cliff?"

Wearily, he shook his head. "I don't think so. How do you get

anywhere with a person who never says anything? I don't even
know if he listened to me."

The missionary thought that would be the end of it, but it
wasn't. Isaac and Albert were back again several days later. Albert
wanted the missionary to talk to him again about the things of
God, to repeat what he had said about salvation.

"And God will keep me from sin?" he asked incredulously.

" 'There hath no temptation taken you but such as is common
to man; but God is faithful, who will not suffer you to be tempted
above that ye are able; but will with the temptation also make a
way of escape, that ye may be able to bear it,' " McComb quoted,
turning to I Corinthians 10:30.

Albert wanted to know more and for the first time the missionary
thought he could see interest. Still, there was no indication that he was
even close to making a decision. It was not until they were at the
door and ready to leave that the young Indian took the tract from
his pocket.

"I want to pray the prayer on the back, here," he told McComb,
pointing to the prayer that acknowledged him a sinner and asked
God to save him. They knelt in the kitchen and Albert Tait confessed
his sin and gave his heart to Christ.

Unlike his cousin, who tried so hard to help him become a
Christian, only to fall back into sin himself a few months later,
Albert went on faithfully with the Lord. A graduate of the Indian
Bible School at La Ronge, Saskatchewan, he is now a teacher and
principal at the Indian Bible School at Island Lake, Manitoba.

Chapter 2

Picking roots or plowing for souls?

Life was hard in the area around Meadow Lake, Saskatchewan in 1933 when homesteader Stan Collie was married. The depression had joined hands with a drouth of unprecedented scope and duration to make money as scarce as waters. The wells, pasture and hay land were dry.

Collie found it a struggle just to keep his small herd of cattle together, let alone build it large enough for the ranch he had dreamed of having. For nine years he had nursed those dreams as he proved his homestead and thought of marriage. There was little money to be married on, but nobody had any money in those days. He and Evelyn were married, determined to do together what he had been unable to do alone.

The drouth continued and so did the relentless fight for existence. Neither Stan nor his wife called upon God in those days. They had grown up without any real contact with the church.

Stan Collie's mother had insisted that he go to Sunday school when he was a boy, but that only lasted until he got old enough to make decisions for himself. It was not that he actually opposed the things of God. Instead, he was indifferent to the claims Christ had on his life. Then Evelyn's three brothers hoboed their way to Vancouver and found Christ as their Saviour in a downtown rescue mission. Almost immediately they began to pray for their sister and her husband.

There were three children in the Collie family by this time (there are now eleven) and they were picking up the profanity and vile language of their father. All through the winter of 1936-1937 a growing conviction of sin settled upon Stan Collie. He tried to stop swearing, without success, and like Albert Tait, even turned to reading the Bible. But his casual, undirected reading didn't help him much.

Early that spring a Rev. Fred Smith came to the vicinity from Pennsylvania to hold special meetings in the schoolhouse. He rode over on horseback to invite the Collie family. Stan halfheartedly agreed that they would do so.

He really didn't want to go, he reasoned later. He didn't know why he had let the preacher talk him into saying he would come. He'd a lot rather stay at home.

But it would be good for Evelyn to go. She'd get a chance to get out and see their neighbors. And, he guessed the religion wouldn't hurt her. They said a little religion never hurt anybody.

"I'm too tired to go, Evelyn," he told his wife the next night. "But the preacher was so anxious to get a good crowd that I think you ought to go and take the kids."

The launching of the special meetings coincided with a celebration and boxing match that was being held in Meadow Lake. Collie had a few drinks and went to the fight. It was warm and stuffy in the building and he got sick. He left the ringside and started for home. But he didn't get there. He stumbled, fell into the gutter, and couldn't get up.

"Who's that?" one woman said to her friend as they walked by.

"Oh, that's Stan Collie——drunk again!"

Stan's fogged mind caught the words and they were a goad to his proud heart.

After that happened he began to go to the special meetings occasionally. There wasn't any connection between his getting drunk and his decison to start going to the meetings, he told himself. He drank a little, but he sure wasn't an alcoholic. And aside from that and his swearing and gambling, he didn't think he was so bad. He didn't need saving. Although he would have denied it profanely at the time, the first faint sparks of interest were beginning to glow in his own heart.

He still was determined not to have anything to do with religion personally, but he had to admit that he liked Rev. Smith. It bothered him to see how tireless the genial young minister was. He had to ride eight or ten miles from Meadow Lake on Saturday for visiting, go back to the place in town where he had a room and repeat the long horseback ride on Sunday morning.

"You'd just as well stay with us on Saturday night," he said.
"That's thoughtful of you, Stan."

"And I've got a good horse for you to ride. That old crow
bait you've been using is apt to die under you before you get where
you're going."

Stan said nothing to Evelyn about it, but he had difficulty in
thinking about anything else all day. He didn't know what had been
the matter with him asking that preacher to stay with them on Saturday
nights. Smith would be after him again about the Lord. If he had
it to do over again, Stan thought, he would have kept his mouth
shut.

Fred Smith came back to the Collie homestead late in the
afternoon and, as his apprehensive host had known he would, he
started to talk about Stan's need to turn his life over to Jesus Christ.
He scarcely waited until supper was over and the chores were done.

Just before midnight April 17, 1937 Stan Collie finally saw
what was wrong with his own life. He realized that he was a con-
demned sinner whom Christ had died to save. There in the kitchen
of his own home one of the first evangelical missionaries of modern
times to the Indians in northern Saskatchewan and co-founder of
the Northern Canada Evangelical Mission (with Art Tarry and
John Penner) made a decision for Christ.

Minutes later his wife did the same.

*   *   *

Collie's interest in the souls of the Canadian Indians came in
a devious way. Although he had been born and raised around them,
he had never thought much about them or their needs. Like the lakes
and the moose and the beaver, they were there. That was as far
as his interest went.

Even after his conversion the Indians didn't figure in his thinking.
He went out with Smith on visitation whenever he could, and later he
and Evelyn held a Sunday school in their home. The next two
summers he made the rounds of farms and ranches in the immediate
area for the Canadian Sunday School Mission recruiting children for
their summer camping program. His newly-awakened concern for
souls was centered upon his own race.

Then he went to a missionary conference in Saskatoon and
was confronted with the dreadful responsibility of Christians towards
the pagan peoples of the world. After one of the sessions, at which
a representative of the Sudan Interior Mission showed slides, he
stayed behind.

"Those pictures you showed tonight were old, weren't they?"
he asked uneasily.

The speaker stopped packing his equipment.

"About a year old, I suppose. Most of the continent of Africa is filled with people like you saw tonight."

Collie was staggered.

"What's the prospects of getting out there as a missionary?" he asked, impulsively.

The other man's eyes narrowed. "How old are you, Mr. Collie?"

"Thirty-two."

"Are you married?"

Collie hadn't realized that would make any difference. He didn't know that the fact that he had a family could influence a mission board, or that they required Bible school or college training for prospective candidates.

"I'm sure the Lord has a place for you somewhere, Mr. Collie," the speaker said as kindly as possible. "But I think you had better forget about Africa."

During the following winter one of Stan's Christian brothers-in-law made a trip north with an old trapper. He came back in the spring with fascinating stories of the North.

"Ile a la Crosse and Patuanak are big settlements, Stan. At Patuanak hundreds of Indians come in during the summer to sell their furs. Most of them camp around the Trading Post until time to go back to their trap lines in the fall."

Stan Collie began to think about the Indians. He knew that the first missionaries had come with the French traders more than a hundred years before. His brother-in-law had told him about the large, well kept churches at both Ile a la Crosse and Patuanak. But he knew as well that Christ had not become a vital force in the lives of any of them. Quite a number of them claimed to belong to one religious system or another, but they didn't seem to know what it meant to take Christ as their personal Saviour. They didn't know that they had to forsake their old ways and the sin that blighted their lives.

A month or so later Stan was picking roots from newly broken ground for a neighbor when the burden for the Indians overwhelmed him. How could he spend his time picking up roots when there was the virgin soil of men's souls to plow? At the moment he had no idea of the difficulty he would face in such an undertaking.

When he got home that night he posed the question to his wife.

"Evelyn," he said, "how do you think you'd like being a missionary's wife?"

If there was any hesitation or doubt in her voice, he didn't note it. "I guess it would be all right."

From that moment on all he could think about was getting into the roadless area to the north and seeing conditions for himself. He wanted to visit these people God had placed so heavily on his heart. He wanted to look for a place to work.

The opportunity came unexpectedly.

Stan had sold a wagon to a farmer for $16.00 and the man surprised him by paying cash. A few days later two itinerant traders from the North stopped in Meadow Lake.

"Sure, we'll take you with us," one of them told him in broken English. "All we ask is that you bring your own grub and gear and do your share of the work." His eyes narrowed. "It isn't easy, this travel in the North."

Stan's first outfit was Spartan. He had a grub box with $16.00 worth of supplies, mosquito netting, some blankets and a piece of old canvas about eight feet square to serve as a tent.

They skirted the shore of Ile a La Crosse Lake.

He soon discovered what the trader meant about travel in the North being difficult. He also learned why they had been so quick to take him along. Fifty miles north of Meadow Lake they camped on the Beaver River long enough to build the big skiffs they needed for hauling their freight. The work was as heavy and the hours as long as any he had ever put in on the ranch.

Once the boats were built they loaded them with freight and started down river. They skirted the shore of long, treacherous Ile a la Crosse Lake, stopped at the settlement of the same name, and finally reached Patuanak. There, he found that everything his brother-in-law had told him about the Indians was true.

"You can go on with us," the trader said, "but we won't be coming back this way."

So Stan Collie turned back.

There were no converts on that trip. Actually, all the trip produced for him was a burden and some good opportunities to share Christ. But he knew when he saw those Indian settlements that this was God's place for him.

"I don't think I ever had such a blessed time in my life as I did on that trip," he wrote years later. "Just being alone with the Lord in the wilderness.   .   .   ."

Chapter 3

"They don't know Jesus, Mom."

The next summer Stan Collie made a trip by boat to Buffalo Narrows, an Indian and Metis settlement north of Ile a la Crosse and just as isolated. He made arrangements for a little fishing caboose on Churchill Lake in the settlement, and in October started north with his wife and five children and his wife's eighteen year old brother.

They loaded what furniture and clothing they had in a neighbor's wagon, along with a sizeable supply of flour and sugar, and started the long trek north. Evelyn Collie thought they would be in Buffalo Narrows two or three days after they left Meadow Lake, so she packed all the clothes except those the children had on. Stan went ahead to Beauval 120 miles or more northeast of Meadow Lake and made arrangements to secure the big scow that would take them the rest of the way, while the neighbor brought the family and their belongings.

Evelyn's estimate of the length of their trip soon proved to be far too optimistic. For a week the Collie family lived in a small tent at Beauval and cooked over a camp fire.

The day they began to load the scow for the down-river trip the weather changed. The bright fall sun gave way to a dull, dripping sky and a cold that chilled the bones. The rising wind scuffed little white caps on the river and sighed mournfully around the tent the Collies had moved from the river bank to the stern of their barge.

The cold increased later in the day, but they scarcely noted it. A certain exhilaration took hold of all of them. At last the waiting was over. They would be heading for Buffalo Narrows with the dawn.

The two men were content to stretch out on the barge and let the weariness seep from their tired bodies, but Evelyn was concerned that the clothing and bed clothes of the children were damp.

"If there was just some way of drying them," she said.

"They'll dry out tomorrow when the sun starts to shine," Stan assured her. "Jim or I can rig up a clothes line for you."

She undressed the children to their underwear and put the driest bedding on their beds. She and Stan lay down on their bed, fully clothed, and Jim stretched his bedroll out on the deck near the stove. The cold built during the night and falling rain drummed steadily on the canvas shelter over them, but they were all so tired they were only faintly aware of it.

Jim was the first to know of the calamity that had befallen them.

"Stan! Evelyn!" he shouted. "We're swamped!"

Instantly they leaped out of bed into icy water ankle deep. In the pre-dawn darkness they could hear the river pouring over the side of the boat.

"The children!" Evelyn Collie cried.

Stan grabbed two, Jim grabbed two and Evelyn snatched up the baby. They sloshed to the side of the scow and scrambled out onto a river bank white and slippery with snow. The fall rain had turned to the season's first snowstorm during the night. Wet snow clung to their faces and soaked their thin jackets as they scrambled up the river bank.

"Stan!" Evelyn cried in sudden desperation. "What are we going to do?"

"There's an Indian home over here!" he shouted.

The Cree woman, who could not speak English, took Mrs. Collie and the children into her little cabin and built a fire to warm them. The men, meanwhile, ran back down to the river to save what they could.

Boxes of books and clothing were hurriedly passed to eager hands on the river bank. The trunks were piled beside them to serve as a platform for the thousand pounds of flour and two hundred pounds of sugar that had been so carefully stowed aboard the afternoon before. Indian men who had never seen the Collies to know who they were, struggled frantically with bedding and mattresses and gear in an attempt to save what they could. The work that had begun in the darkness of early morning was finished in chill gray light of day. At last, exhausted, the little group of men lifted the last box ashore and dragged off to their homes.

Indian men struggled frantically with gear.

Later in the day Evelyn Collie accompanied her discouraged husband to the river bank in an attempt to assess the damage.

"We'll be able to use the scow again," Stan said, his voice thin and taut. "But a lot of this is no good any more."

Some of the books were soaked until the pages stuck together and the covers warped; the water had ruined their accordion and ran the colors together on a lot of their clothes. And some of their precious stores of food were destroyed.

"Look at our sugar," he continued. "It's like syrup."

"We'll put it in tubs and save it anyway," his wife retorted. "We can use it like that as long as it lasts."

The damage to their belongings and stores was already done. Now they were faced with an immediate problem.

"We have to have a place to live until we can get our things dry," Stan explained to one of the Cree men who could speak English.

"My friend is away on his trap line," the Indian said. "You can live in his house until you are ready to go on."

They moved into the Indian cabin and for the next ten days kept fires going in both the wood burning heater and cook stove to dry out their clothes and bedding. Once that was done they re-loaded the scow and set off for Buffalo Narrows. They made their way down the Beaver River, across Ile a la Crosse Lake, stopped in the settlement with friends for a night or two, and went on to their destination. It was after dark when they pulled up at the Buffalo Narrows' dock.

That was the night of November 4. The next morning the wind was driving deep-throated swells across the lake and freezing the spray on the dock. No boats were venturing out in the gale, let alone one as cumbersome and shallow of draft as the scow the Collie's had arrived in. Had they not reached the settlement the night before they would have been forced to camp wherever they were and wait for the wind to go down. On November 6 when they got up and looked out Churchill Lake was frozen over as far as they could see.

"Look out there," Stan said, his voice choking. "God got us here at the last possible day we could have travelled. If this had come a few days sooner——"

Evelyn shuddered. She, too, had been thinking that very thing.

Although they had spent their first night in Buffalo Narrows with a family they had just met, they wanted to get into their own place as soon as possible. So, as soon as breakfast was finished Stan went down to the place where the fishing caboose had been when he made arrangements to use it.

There was no sign of it anywhere.

In the Hudson Bay Store he asked about the man who rented it to him.

"He was in and got some supplies a couple of weeks ago," the manager said. "I understand he's gone fishing."

"What about that caboose he had down by the lake?" Stan asked.

The manager turned and questioned a lad by the stove in Cree.

"He moved that out to where he was fishing," he told Stan a moment later.

"But he rented it to me."

The Hudson Bay man shrugged.

"I guess he figured he needed it worse than you did."

The Collies stayed with their hosts until they found a large log workshop that would serve as their home. There they had the first Sunday school with as many as 32 children on Sunday mornings. In the evening they were hosts to 15 or 20 adults.

*   *   *

Most of the trading in the isolated North is done in the winter. At the time the Collies were in Buffalo Narrows the * 'cat trains' were great sleds drawn by teams of six or eight horses. The hotel or 'stopping house' as it was called then, had a big barn where the teams were cared for. Usually the drivers would stay for a week or so, resting their sturdy animals before starting the long haul back to Meadow Lake.

---

* Today they are series of large bobsleds hooked in tandem and pulled by a Caterpillar tractor.

Stan Collie got a job cleaning out the barn. It didn't pay very well, but he had a large family to take care of, and no other source of income. Later he got some nets and an old boat and did some commercial fishing, but his chief responsibility—his reason for being there—was to fish for the hearts of men.

While Stan and Evelyn Collie were facing the problems of providing for their family and reaching those around them for Christ, their oldest children were facing problems of another sort. Those they went to school with swore at them and threw rocks at them whenever they saw them on the streets. The bitterness in the hearts of some parents exploded into action by their children.

"Devils!" boys and girls alike would shout, shrilly. "Devils! Go back where you came from!"

Geraldine and Billy were both terrified.

This went on for several months until a couple of Metis boys a little older than they were felt sorry for them and took it upon themselves to protect them. They took to walking home from school with them at night and stopping by the Collie house for them in the morning. That changed the situation considerably. Occasionally remarks were snarled at the missionary's children from hating lips, but there was no more rock throwing, no more chasing them to the very door of their home.

However, all the children felt the hot breath of persecution in one way or another.

On one occasion, three of the boys were taken down the basement and backed against the wall by much bigger fellows. Then, spreading out their arms they nailed their sleeves to the wall.

"Look at them!" they taunted. "They're little Jesus'!"

The teacher heard the commotion and came down to find the terrified children where their tormentors had nailed them. Grinning, he turned away as though he had not seen it.

When one of the younger girls was starting to school a couple of Metis girls spit in her face and tried to get her to blaspheme against Christ. Each time she refused they would spit in her face again.

Beth came in, sobbing out her story. Evelyn Collie's temper flared. She was just waiting for her daughter to finish telling her what had happened so she could dash out and accost the girls who had been abusing Beth.

But when her daughter looked up there was no anger in her soft eyes.

"I feel so sorry for them, Mom," she said simply. "They don't *know* Jesus!"

*   *   *

The Collies had five children when they moved from Meadow Lake. And Evelyn went south to the hospital there when Kenny was born. Beth, however, was expected to put in her appearance the last part of April.

"I don't want to go out this time, Stan," she said. "I'd have to leave before break-up and wouldn't be able to come back until the truck road from Meadow Lake to Beauval is good and the rivers and lakes are free of ice. I don't want to be away from you and the children so long."

So, it was decided that she would remain in Buffalo Narrows for this particular confinement.

Not long before the baby was due a French family moved to the settlement and the wife came over and stayed 10 days after the baby was born. She was excellent help.

Beth put in her appearance April 27. May 10 Evelyn insisted on going out to the garden to help Stan.

"It's such a lovely day," she explained.

"You'd better stay in the house, Evelyn," he told her.

"It's not going to hurt me to be out here for a little while," she countered. "I just want to be out in the sun and get some fresh air."

A short time later he turned to her again.

"Don't you think you'd better go in now?" he asked.

"I will in a little while. I'm not going to hurt myself. I'll quit when I get tired."

An hour or so later he again suggested that she go back to the cabin, but again she refused. It was not until he left the garden late in the afternoon that she went, too. Fatigue lined her face and her cheeks were sallow. Dark circles shadowed the hollows beneath her eyes.

"Evelyn," Stan said, "you'd better go lie down and let me get supper."

This time she did not argue with him and did as he suggested. Not long afterwards she started to hemorrhage and continued through the night. As soon as the Department of Natural Resources short wave radio network (that interlaces the Saskatchewan north) went on the air Stan radioed the doctor at Ile a la Crosse.

"I should see her," the doctor said, "but there's no chance of getting over there."

It was break-up time. There was floating ice in the lakes. Boats were still pulled up on shore, useless until the water-ways cleared, and the aircraft all around the North were waiting until they could be operated safely on floats again. The emergency had happened at one of the two times each year when isolation is complete.

The doctor outlined exactly what they should do.

"I'm sorry," he concluded, "but that's all the help I can give you. Over and out."

They did everything the doctor advised, but the bleeding did not stop. Evelyn grew steadily weaker until she could scarcely talk. Then, about six o'clock in the evening, she reached over and grasped her distraught husband's hand.

"Stan," she scarcely whispered. "I'm going to sleep."

But they both knew it was not sleep that she was talking about. Her fingers relaxed and she closed her eyes.

Stan Collie dropped to his knees beside the bed and began to talk to God. He had prayed often since that night back on his Meadow Lake ranch when he made his decision for Christ. He had prayed about an avenue of service, about getting to the North to see the need, and about moving to Buffalo Narrows. He had prayed after their scow swamped at Beauval ruining so many of their belongings. And for a house when he wasn't able to get the one he had rented at Buffalo Narrows. But as he knelt in anguish beside his wife's bed it seemed that he had never prayed before—that there weren't even words to voice the desperate petitions of his heart.

"Dear God," he prayed aloud. "Heal Evelyn's body! . . . . Spare her life! . . ."

There was more. Much more. But Stan's was the almost wordless crying out of an anguished heart.

Much later Evelyn was to write of the experience.

"I've never had anything like that happen to me before or since. The hemorrhaging stopped and my strength returned immediately. It was wonderful!"

*   *   *

There were joys as well as hardships for the Collies at Buffalo Narrows. From the very beginning there were results. The trip Stan made to see about moving his family to the settlement resulted in the salvation of a boy fifteen or sixteen years old.

The lad started out bravely enough, making his stand against the things of the world, against the opposition in his own home, and that of the established order in Buffalo Narrows. Even now, many years later, Stan Collie believes the conversion was genuine. But the pressures new converts face in such a settlement are enough to wilt the faith and determination of all but the strongest. This young man could not withstand the persecution that was levelled at him and finally he slipped back into the sins of his old life.

Rene Caisse however, was different.

He was little more than a toddler living with his grandmother when the Collies moved to Buffalo Narrows and built a cabin near her home. Without discipline at home, he grew up a savage little creature with a profane tongue, a quick temper, and all the cunning of a clever mind. He was fed on his grandmother's unrelenting hatred of the Collies and Tarrys and the gospel they preached until he felt he was performing a service when he bounced a rock off some unsuspecting child's head or taunted one of the adults.

"Go back where you belong, you devils!" he would screech, always keeping an eye on an escape route lest they should lose their tempers and start after him (which they never did). "You devils! Devils!" And the air would ring with profanity from the lips of one so young he didn't even know the meaning of the epithets he hurled at them.

Finally Rene tired of his campaign against the missionaries' children and even began to play with them occasionally. A Christian teacher took over the Buffalo Narrows school and befriended the Metis lad.

One summer Rene surprised them all by agreeing to go out to Bible Camp with the older Collie and Tarry youngsters. Who first suggested it isn't quite clear, but very likely, the chief reason he went to camp can be found in the fact that the school teacher and his wife Mr. and Mrs. Philip Listoe offered to pay his way if he would go. (The same couple helped him considerably in a financial way when he was going to high school in Caronport, Saskatchewan.)

At camp young Rene made a decision for Christ. But when he returned to Buffalo Narrows he wouldn't let anyone else know he was a Christian. His language cleared up and his life was different, but he gave no indication by his own words that he was a believer.

"I want to live for Christ," he would tell Art Tarry or the Collies, or the Listoes, with whom he lived months at a time when his grandmother was out on her trap line. But it was months before he dared to stand up and let his old friends and associates know that he was now a Christian.

The Christians who knew him were disappointed in his lack of courage and privately thought that it wouldn't be long until they wouldn't be able to tell him from all the rest of the young men in the settlement. But they reckoned without the work God had done in Rene's young heart. When he finally made his public stand the persecution that is so effective against so many was directed at him. Yet he did not waver once, to the lasting disappointment of his grandmother who loved him as her son.

He went through Grade 8 at Buffalo Narrows, to the surprise of many, went to Caronport with the urging and financial help of Philip and Joyce Listoe, and graduated from high school and Bible school. He went on to prepare himself to teach and is now a teacher and a stalwart Christian in a semi-isolated settlement north of Prince Albert.

There are hardships, disappointments and often failures in places that are least expected to bring discouragement to the missionary. But it is Rene Caisse and the others like him who make the work so worthwhile for the missionaries in the North—men and women who make decisions for the Saviour, who drive their roots deep into the Word of God in spite of opposition, and who live exemplary, fruitful lives for Christ.

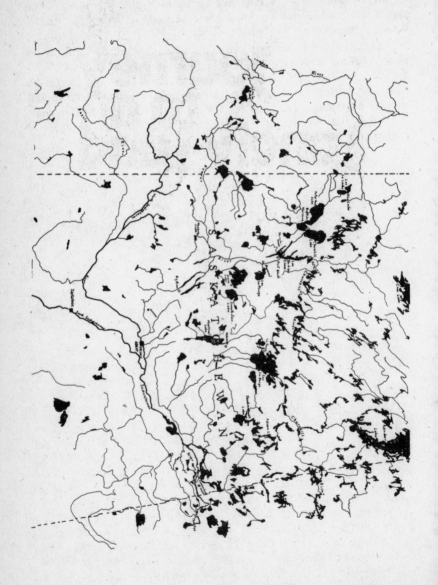

Chapter 4

We don't need much of an organization.

"Winter has finally loosed its icy grip," Stan Collie wrote in an early issue of *Northern Lights* shortly after break-up. "Ptarmigan and snowbirds have followed the migrating caribou to the summer homes in the Barrens. Great flocks of geese and swans and cranes have rested briefly with us and continued their northward journeys. But the forests around the lake are not quiet these days. Our own song birds have returned and the ducks are making ready once again to set up housekeeping in the marshes nearby. The crows and blackbirds are chortling noisily, and their discordant voices bring a smile to the heart that spring is here.

"For months our lakes and rivers have been stilled by ice and snow. Now, however, they are beginning to yield, though somewhat reluctantly it seems to the impatient watcher, to the sunshine and warm May winds.

"The vast sheet of yard-thick ice that covered Peter Pond Lake for so long has begun to break up at last. First it breaks into floating islands driven this way and that by changing winds. Then, rumbling and roaring like a distant volcano or like the incessant dynamite charges of a road crew to the south of us, the ice splits into smaller floes. It piles high against islands and rocky points ripping out docks and heaving rocks up on shore. It jams river mouths and clogs bays, shifting noisily with the caprice of the change-

It piles high against islands and rocky points.

able spring winds. Once the disintegration begins it continues without letup until the last chunk of ice has melted into the lake.

"The winter highways of dog teams, trucks and 'cat trains' disappear, and those very important vehicles of travel are put away for another summer season.

"Activity in the settlements increases feverishly. Canoes are repaired, boats are caulked and painted, and the bush planes, those aptly named 'pack mules of the North,' are once more mounted on floats.

"Even now the Indians and Metis are beginning to drift in from their wilderness trapping grounds with their winter's catch of furs. They will be congregated at the trading posts for most of the short summer season. If the season was good they will be in new tents with new canoes or outboard motors. Unless, that is, they spend their substance on cheap liquor and the inevitable gambling that goes on in such encampments.

"To the missionary the Northland summer presents a great opportunity—a tremendous and awesome responsibility. Consider it for a moment! Practically the entire population of an area comprising three-quarters of our Dominion of Canada gathered together into a few score settlements. That is our opportunity! A people, living at our very back door who have been denied the true Gospel. That is our responsibility!"

Stan and Evelyn Collie saw three such break-ups come while they labored alone at Buffalo Narrows. They saw the opportunities of three brief summers, hearts aching because they could not take full advantage of them.

In 1942 they built a little frame church and held regular services in it for two years. Then in 1944, shortly after the fourth break-up they witnessed at Buffalo Narrows, Stan went down to Meadow Lake to meet with several officials of the Canadian Sunday School Mission and others who were interested in reaching the Indian tribes of the North for Christ.

The meeting resulted in a brief, but very important period of support by the Canadian Sunday School Mission for the Collies and several others who felt called to take the gospel to the isolated regions of northern Saskatchewan.

*   *   *

In 1939, about the same time God first began to deal with Stan Collie about the area he was now serving in, He began to speak to the heart of another individual. Art Tarry, a second year student at Briercrest Bible Institute, began to feel the burden for the unreached Indian tribes who hunted, trapped and fished in the roadless areas of their land. However, the way didn't seem open to him on graduation so he went with the Canadian Sunday School Mission for a year and a half.

Then, getting married, he took a pastorate for another three years. But all the while the cry of the Indian people was still ringing in his ears.

Finally, in the early months of 1944 his wife said, "Art, if you still want to go north, I'm ready to go with you."

He learned of the work the Collies were doing and contacted them. It wasn't long until arrangements had been made for the Tarrys to go to Buffalo Narrows to help the Collies. Two single girls, Misses Olmstead and Kennedy spent some time at the same settlement before going on to the hard and lonely village of La Loche to work alone. And Norwegian Nils Folkvord, a giant of a man both physically and mentally, was sent by the Canadian Sunday School Mission to La Ronge.

And John Penner, a close personal friend of the Tarrys from his Briercrest days, was also getting restless in the pulpit he was filling. He, too, was being drawn to the North by the irresistible force of the Holy Spirit. It wasn't long until he and his wife took up residence at Ile a la Crosse.

While the assistance of the Canadian Sunday School Mission was vital the first two years of the expanded ministry north of Meadow Lake, it soon became apparent that God had other plans for the work among the Indians. For one thing, it was a cumbersome arrangement. Headquarters was far away and the men who, organizationally speaking, should be making the decisions, knew but little of the needs or opportunities.

The work in southern Canada was set up on sharply divided provincial lines. This, too, failed to fit the needs of the North. Already Tarry, Collie and the others were looking with anxious hearts at Alberta, Manitoba and Ontario.

Another, and not inconsiderable factor, was the fact that the CSSM had a very difficult time in supplying funds for the Indian workers that were already there. Any expansion would have been virtually impossible under the existing arrangement with them.

"I can't understand it, Stan," Mr. Aikenhead, General Superintendent of the Canadian Sunday School Mission, told Collie at a meeting in the spring of 1946 after it became apparent that something else would have to be worked out. "Wherever I present our work I always tell about the ministry you people have among the northern Indians. But I've never once had anyone give me any money towards it."

After long and prayerful consideration by both the CSSM Board and the northern missionaries it was decided that two separate organizations would be the best answer to the problem.

One afternoon shortly after the decision was reached Tarry and Collie were sawing wood. As they sawed, or stopped to catch their breath, they talked about their next moves.

"We don't need much of an organization," one of them said. "Just a few men who are acquainted with the Indian work and the problems and have a burden for it."

"That's right. We don't want to create a big mission or get ourselves bogged down in red tape."

They discussed it for a few minutes.

"Of course," someone added, "we'll have to incorporate in order to issue receipts to our donors for income tax purposes."

"And if we do that, we've got to have a name."

It wasn't long until a name was suggested. The Northern Canada Evangelical Mission.

The first year of the work was unspeakably hard. The new mission received only $300. One man of God spoke bluntly to Art Tarry about it.

"You fellows are never going to get anywhere. Your mission will die an early death."

But God withheld the knowledge of the hardships of the future from them, as they set up their little group. Once they had decided upon a name they plunged into the legal details of organization. They appointed a board, and got committees to work drawing up a constitution and by-laws. It wasn't long until they were ready to look for new missionaries.

"What are we going to do when we get letters expressing interest?" someone asked in one of the early board meetings.

"Other missions have application blanks and require references and a physical examination. We ought to do the same."

A motion was passed and still another committee appointed to develop the necessary papers.

Chapter 5

Busted suitcase and burned bridges.

While Anne Koop was still in Bible school the Lord spoke to her heart about the mission field. And when she graduated in 1945 she attended Wycliffe's Summer Institute of Linguistics, determined to go to the North to work among Canada's largely neglected Indians.

"What mission board will you be under?" she was asked, on occasion.

Twin spots of color stained her cheeks.

"I don't know yet."

Actually, she had not been able to find a mission that was doing Indian work in the area she was concerned about. The Collies and Tarrys were out under the Canadian Sunday School Mission, but that was all she was able to learn. So as far as she was concerned the founding of the NCEM was an answer to prayer.

She contacted them immediately and received a cautiously worded letter in reply.

One afternoon there was a knock on the door of the Meadow Lake house where the Collies were staying temporarily while Stan was working with the other men on the organizational details of the Mission. Stan Collie opened it to see a slight, attractive young lady standing there with a bulging suitcase in her hand.

"Are you Mr. Collie?" she asked timidly.

"That's right. Won't you come in?"

"I'm Anne Koop," she explained, smiling shyly. "I've come to work with the mission."

"Here we were going to be like the big foreign missionary societies and screen all our applicants," Stan said, still chuckling about it years later, "and this little slip of a Mennonite girl came barging in before we even had our red tape set up. She never did fill out an application or get accepted. We just sent her to Buffalo Narrows and put her to work."

Stan Collie found her a ride north by truck a few days after her arrival in Meadow Lake. It was just after dinner when the big vehicle, piled high with freight, stopped at the door. Momentarily she stood on the porch looking at the truck that was to take her north.

"Is everything all right?" Evelyn Collie asked.

"Oh, yes," she said quickly, swallowing at the lump that swelled, unbidden, in her throat. "Everything's fine."

The driver loaded her baggage and she climbed up into the seat beside him. The Collies watched them rumble noisily away.

"What do you think, Evelyn?" Stan asked, pensively after a minute or so of silence.

"She is so positive that the Lord called her to work in the North," his wife answered, trying to put down her own uneasiness over their first new missionary. "But she seems so tiny——so frail."

And they knew the demands that would be made upon her. But there was no chance of advising her against the North, no way of convincing her that she should serve where less would be required of her, physically.

In the seat of the big truck Anne Koop was beginning to relax as she saw that the road was smooth and quite well travelled. This wasn't so bad yet, she reasoned. Not nearly what she had expected. Of course she was going to the end of the road and beyond. From the place where the truck stopped she would have to go to Ile a la Crosse by boat.

"And when you get to the settlement there," Stan had told her again just before she left, "have the DNR field officer radio the Mission. The plane will come over from Buffalo Narrows and get you."

She remembered smiling at him bravely and hoping he wasn't aware of the fact that she had never ridden in a plane before.

At the edge of the little Indian community of Green Lake the driver left the well travelled road for what appeared to be a trail through the bush. It was scarcely wide enough for one vehicle and still deeply rutted from the spring rains. She looked at it with growing apprehension. At last she could no longer contain herself.

Are you sure this is the right road?

"Are you sure this is the right road?" she asked him.

Disdain flickered in his dark eyes. "Lady, I've made this trip a hundred times."

"Oh," she retorted weakly. "Oh, I'm sorry."

She sat back in silence, jouncing painfully with every lurch of the truck and mentally trying to count off the miles.

'Surely we ought to be getting close to the settlement,' she told herself. 'It can't possibly be more than a few miles.'

And then the truck engine sputtered without warning.

"What was that?" she gasped.

The trucker worked the throttle, but the laboring motor did not respond.

"Out of gas," he said cryptically.

He got out and disappeared somewhere. Out of gas! Her heart stood still. As far as she could see ahead the trail went into the bush. For all she knew they might be 50 miles from their destination. And she had no idea how many dozens of miles they had travelled since leaving Green Lake with its houses, its stores and its filling stations. She had never realized what a wonderful thing a filling station was until that very moment.

Out of gas! And in a place like this!

The driver would have to walk for help. And it was so late he couldn't possibly get back before dark. That meant she'd have to spend the night in the truck alone. Suddenly she wondered if all the stories she had heard about wolves and bears were true.

She had been so upset by the knowledge that they had run out of gas that she hadn't thought to wonder what the driver had been doing since they stopped. Now he opened his door and crawled back under the steering wheel.

"W-w-what are you going to do?" she asked, her voice thin and almost apologetic.

"Get goin'," he told her brusquely. "I always have to stop about here and fill up from that barrel I've got in the back."

Anne Koop breathed a prayer of thanksgiving and relief.

The road north had been rough on high ground, but now as they entered the muskeg it seemed bottomless. The driver shifted into low gear in one particularly bad stretch. Still the truck's forward motion slowed. Finally it ground to a halt.

"I was afraid of that!" He probably would have sworn had it not been for his slight, ashen-faced passenger. "You'd just as well relax. We'll be here for a little while."

She watched him cut a number of straight, slender trees and drag them across the road, branches and all, to make a crude corduroy. When he had finished he got back in the truck cab and started the engine.

"This might be a bit rough," he told her.

With that he depressed the gas pedal and let out the clutch. The cumbersome, heavily-loaded vehicle lurched forward.

"Hang on!" he shouted above the roar of the motor. "Hang on!"

The truck bucked wildly as they roared across the piece of corduroy to the dry ground on the other side.

"Well," he said, obviously pleased with himself and thankful that this part of the road had been negotiated, "we made it."

Anne Koop thought of her aching back and throbbing muscles. "Yes," she said without complaining. "We made it."

The driver must have realized how weary she was and tried to cheer her up. Every now and then he glanced her way.

"Are you still with me?"

Her teeth chattered and she tightened her hold on the dash board as she answered him.

Finally, at eleven o'clock that night, they stopped in a little Indian village.

"This isn't much of a place for a lady to stay," the trucker apologized, pulling up before the ramshackle building that contained a few rooms travelers could rent, "but there just isn't anything else."

"If it's got a bed in it, that's all I ask," she said wearily.

She had supposed she was too tired and ached too much to sleep, but she closed her eyes. The next thing she knew, it was morning.

Anne was up and ready to leave the little settlement several hours before the trucker would be going. Curious to see her first Indian village, she walked around, seeing the little makeshift homes of the people who had been on her heart so long.

Quite unexpectedly she came upon a huge cemetery on the edge of the clearing. Stunned for a moment by the scene before her, she remained motionless, staring at the mounds of earth that represented so much sorrow, so much despair and hopelessness. Then, as though drawn by some hidden force, she moved forward to stand before one of the graves, marked by a pagan fetish. Religion had been among the people for almost a century. Most of the villagers, she had been told, would say they were its followers. Yet in all those years the old pagan customs had not been taken from their hearts.

"Lord," she asked aloud, "where are all of these souls now?"

Yet there was no need for the question. She already knew what the answer was. The same answer was written on the unhappy faces she met on the paths.

"Dear Father," she continued, praying in renewed dedication, "my life is yours. Use me to bring some of these dear ones to Christ."

And at that moment the tortuous ride of the day before became as nothing. The rest of her life, God willing, was to be used to minister to these Indian people. Even though the responsibility was sobering, and there would be hardships, discouragements and failures, there was a song in her heart as she went back to the hotel.

By noon the driver had unloaded the portion of his load that stayed in the settlement and was ready for the last leg of the journey. This time it was to be only a few more miles. He stopped near the river and got out. "This is as far as I go, Lady," he told her, helping her get her suitcase. "That scow'll be leaving for Ile a la Crosse in a few minutes. You can cross with them."

The cumbersome, sluggish craft had scarcely pulled away from the dock when a sudden, driving shower hit them.

"Here," one of the men said, breaking out a tarp. "We can get under this."

Although Anne and the other passengers kept fairly dry, everything else aboard was soaked.

By this time she was a seasoned traveller.

Once they reached Ile a la Crosse she inquired for the DNR office, walked over to it and sent a message to Buffalo Narrows. The pilot had been expecting her as the result of a previous radio call from Stan Collie, and had gassed, ready to take off.

She had only to wait for the wagon that had been dispatched to bring the freight and luggage up from the boat and she would be ready for the short hop to the Buffalo Narrows station. This was one portion of the trip she had been looking forward to.

Minutes before the plane arrived the wagon stopped with the freight and she moved towards it with the other passengers.

"Oh, oh," somebody murmured, "a broken suitcase."

Her heart caught. Without even seeing it she knew who the broken suitcase belonged to. Hers had been inexpensive and not too sturdy to begin with. Crammed as it was with all her personal belongings, it wouldn't have taken much to cause the cardboard sides to give way. Everything in it was soaked. She groaned inwardly.

But that was not the end of her troubles. The plane arrived and the missionary pilot wanted to leave her suitcase behind.

"I'm sorry," he told her, " but the plane's too small. We can't take any luggage."

She stared at him. This wasn't real! It couldn't be!

"But I've got to have my suitcase," she pleaded.

"I'm sorry, but we've got to keep the load down," he tried to explain. "If we don't, we're not going to be able to get off the water."

Her eyes reflected her dismay. "But I won't even have a change of clothes," she protested.

Their eyes met. And for an instant or two loneliness and homesickness swept over her in a flood. It was as though she suddenly was friendless and completely alone.

"Well——" He relented a little. "Pick out what you absolutely can't do without."

"I've already done that," she insisted, tears trembling on her eyelashes. "I don't have a thing in that suitcase I can spare."

He surveyed her critically.

"You are sort of skinny," he observed. "We'll put the suitcase in and see what happens."

"Oh, thank you!"

"But if we can't get off, we'll have to leave you, or your suitcase here in Ile a la Crosse."

Fortunately there was wind enough to ruffle the surface of the lake and the little Taylor-craft was able to get into the air.

"That was the first time I ever praised the Lord for being skinny and under-nourished," she told friends later.

"Welcome to Buffalo Narrows," the pilot said as he helped her ashore at the settlement that had so recently become the head-quarters for the young mission.

"I'm here to stay," she replied as the weariness of the long trip engulfed her. "I've burned all of my bridges behind me." She thought back over the events of the past few days. "I have absolutely no desire to retrace my footsteps."

*   *   *

The way north has always been arduous for those who have gone with the message of Christ. To be sure, it is a bit easier these days with the more wide-spread use of aircraft. Some of the mission-aries have power toboggans to use in the place of dog teams and power saws are taking some of the back-breaking work out of cutting fire-wood for the winter. But the isolation, the loneliness, the concern about illness of their children or themselves far from medical assis-tance, and ordinary housekeeping—the tasks of keeping warm and well and with hunger satisfied, things we do so casually in other parts of the country, are still problems of undiminished scope in the North.

Then there is the cold——the nagging, persistent, ever-present cold. Yet, to the missionary who goes north, it is not the cold of winter that causes his concern nearly as much as the icy indifference of the hearts of the people he is trying to reach with the unsearchable riches of Christ.

Chapter 6

"You the passengers for Camsell?"

Some who are called to the Lord's service respond immediately. Others resist for months or years before God is able to bring them to the place of submission. Ray Bradford belongs in neither group. In his senior year of Bible school God laid the burden of the Indian people of Canada upon his heart. But there was a war on that spring of 1941. He was called into the army for four months of active training, and before that was over he joined the active force and spent nearly 5 years overseas.

"All that time the vision of the people of the North stayed with me," he wrote.

And, shortly after he was discharged in 1946 Ray and his bride joined the new mission. At the same time they agreed to go to Camsell Portage, a little Saskatchewan village on the north shores of Lake Athabasca, a stone's throw from the Northwest Territories. Ray gave notice to his Calgary employer and booked passage for two on the one flight a month that left from Edmonton for the Lake Athabasca settlements.

Methodically, his wife Catherine, made preparations to go. They could only carry 40 pounds of luggage each. And that would have to last them nine months until the barge came in with freight.

"I packed away most of our wedding gifts," she remembers, "including all of the electrical appliances and heavy dishes. We gave away some of the gifts we felt would never be used in the North."

Ray and Catherine went to Edmonton a day early and the following morning went out to where they were to take off. Men were busy loading mail, supplies and liquor into a battered old Norseman that looked as though it wouldn't be able to stagger into the air again.

"You the passengers for Camsell, eh?" one of them asked.

"That's right." Ray tried to hide his apprehension at the aircraft they would be riding in.

"Are you going to have room for us?" Catherine put in. Uncertainty colored her voice.

"Oh, sure. On this flight we always make room for our passengers."

They were the only persons going north that month, but there was so much freight they had a difficult time squeezing in.

"We've fixed a seat for you right in the middle of the plane," the pilot said cheerfully, "Where everything can fall on you if we hit rough air."

Ray Bradford looked at his young wife. She smiled happily. This was the day they both had been waiting for, the day that marked the beginning of their service for the Lord.

Some four or five hours later the Norseman nosed down at the little Indian village the missionary couple were going to call their home for the next several years. Everyone in the settlement was down to meet the plane and, unexplainably, the*Indians seemed to know that a missionary was aboard.

Everyone in the settlement was down to meet the plane.

One old fellow with no fingers on either hand came up to Ray. "When are you going to have your first service?" he asked.

---

* On a number of occasions we have come across evidence of the phenomenon known in the North as 'moccasin telegraph,' the bewildering transmission of information from one area to another without benefit of any visible means of communication. Some shrug it off, others are mystified without looking for explanation, and still others believe it to be associated with their pagan religion and spiritism.

They moved into the little cabin Stan had made arrangements for them to use when he was in Camsell several months before. That night Calgary and Edmonton seemed very far away, indeed.

"We've come here a little like Abraham did when God told him to go to a far country, Cathy," Ray said. "We've never been here before, and we don't know what to expect, or what's going to happen."

There was a short silence.

"We don't even know for sure what we're going to do for money. The Mission told us they won't be able to help us, and we don't have much of our own."

She slipped her arm about his waist.

"But we have each other," she said confidently, "and the Lord."

For those who go to live in the North getting wood to burn is a formidable task not left until the last minute. Trees are cut, limbed and piled well in advance. The logs are sawed into 8 foot lengths, hauled back to the cabin to dry, and cut and split for the stove.

Although the Bradfords had come to Camsell Portage to preach the gospel, Ray's first task was to cut wood to fill the yawning mouth of the heating stove. There was no time for delay to get acquainted, no time to find someone to help. It was October and the brief summer period had fled. It was windy and cold and snowing. He climbed the hill behind the little log shack Stan Collie had secured for them, chopped down some green trees, and pulled them down-hill with a rope.

"Can I help you, Ray?" Catherine asked.

"You can bring me that 'Swede saw,' if you want to."

With the Swede saw he cut the wood into short lengths and, because it was green and didn't burn well, he had to split it with an ax. It was slow, gruelling work alone.

It would have been difficult enough had there been plenty of wood nearby, but so far north they were close to the timber line and the trees were scrawny and somewhat scattered. It wasn't long until the missionary couple had burned all the wood nearby and had to go out into the bush for more.

That winter was one of heavy snow, and by the end of November it was five feet deep.

"You can imagine what it's like cutting down trees with the snow practically up to your chin," Ray said, chuckling as he remembered.

By this time he had begun to make friends with some of the

Indians. They would go with him after he had cut the wood into 8 foot lengths and haul it in with their dog teams.

Firewood, they soon discovered, was not the only problem that faced them. They soon learned what it meant to be without money or any regular means of support. They began to understand that it was one thing to speak airily of going wherever the Lord called and undergoing any hardships along the way, and quite another to translate that resolve into day by day living.

"Well, what's for supper tonight?" Ray would ask cheerily, coming in from a cold afternoon on the 'Swede saw.'

"I thought I'd give you a treat tonight and fix some macaroni."

"Just exactly what I wanted."

"Tomorrow morning we'll have porridge," she said.

And, perhaps they would have both porridge and macaroni for the next day's dinner or supper. It was all they had in the house and, for the moment at least, there was little prospect of getting anything more. But there was always something to eat and they never really suffered from a lack of food.

"It is marvelous to see how God provides for us," Ray wrote to friends. "There are times when we can't see how we will possibly get what we need, but we always do, and in some of the most unusual ways. I think God uses the unusual at times so we will be sure to see that He is the One who is providing for our needs."

But with all the difficulties they faced upon arrival in Camsell Portage the Bradfords soon launched into their primary responsibility, that of getting acquainted with the people and beginning to witness to them.

It wasn't long until they became painfully aware of the scope of the task that faced them. As in so much of the North, sectarian missionaries had come with the French traders a hundred years or so before and had staked out vast areas they called their own. Most of the Indians named themselves among their followers, although all but a handful had no concept of what they taught or believed. They had been baptized in their parents' arms and wore the label. Yet they were as pagan and just as lost as any of their ancestors before the white man came.

Fort Chipewyan had a resident religionist. Before the Bradfords came to Camsell he seldom visited the village. Once their presence became known, however, his visits were frequent and pointed.

Some of those who befriended the young missionaries at first no longer spoke to them on the streets. Others apparently still liked them, but no longer opened their homes. Even the children were affected.

Shortly after Ray and Catherine moved to Camsell Portage charming nine year old Noreen became quite friendly. She loved to come over and visit them, and often would pick up the Bible the Bradfords kept on the kitchen table. At first she would just leaf through it. But then she got to reading in one place or another. It became an almost daily occurence for her.

After one of her visits she said to her mother, "Mummy, I'd like to have a Bible just like Mr. Bradford's."

Her mother was furious.

"If you go over to that house again," she threatened. "I'll give you a good beating!"

Several weeks passed and the little girl didn't come back to visit. The Bradfords became concerned.

"Have you seen Noreen lately, Catherine?" Ray asked.

"I've seen her around the settlement, but she hasn't spoken to me. If she sees me she turns away."

"I was afraid that would happen. I think I'll talk to her mother the next time I go out on visitation."

It wasn't long until he was making calls and felt led to stop at Noreen's home. Her mother invited him in, but was cold and distant. Several times he tried to make conversation, but she answered in monosyllables and did not stop working about the kitchen.

"Noreen hasn't been in our home for quite a long while," he said, finally broaching the subject that had brought him there. "And my wife and I feel very badly about it. We love to have her come and see us."

Fire leaped to her eyes and her face flushed a deep crimson.

"Is there some reason why you don't let her come to see us any more?"

Briefly she stopped sweeping, her stare driving through him. Then the words spilled out, angrily.

"You're trying to turn Noreen from her religion!" she exploded. "You're befriending her so you can steal her from her church and from me! . . . . What are you doing up here? Why don't you go back where you belong?"

As she raged at him she wielded the broom faster and faster. He eyed it with some uneasiness, wondering how much it would hurt to get whacked over the head with a broom. She swept right up to his feet, stopped and jabbed a trembling finger under his nose.

"Mr. Bradford!" she stormed, "Noreen will never be allowed to visit in your home again. She was born into our religion, she has lived in our religion, and she's going to die in our religion."

Noreen never did set foot in the Bradford home again. The following winter she contracted meningitis, lost consciousness and died.

"We often wondered," Ray said, "whether in her reading of the Word of God and the few times we talked with her, if she had repented of her sin, or as her mother vowed, if she had indeed died in her religion."

*   *   *

Lake Athabasca is big, dangerous and compelling. It was small wonder that the Bradfords would, on occasion, find themselves in conflict with it.

A year or so after their arrival at Camsell Portage a white trapper by the name of Norman Chopping and his trapper partner were going out to their trap line on the south side of the big lake.

"You should go along, Ray," he said. "We're going to take a canoe across the lake to the river mouth. Joe will take the dogs and walk up the river to the trapline. I'm going to bring the canoe back and charter a plane to take me and our supplies out a little later."

Ray Bradford looked out at the big lake.

"It would be an experience," he said. What he didn't say was that it would also be an opportunity to get better acquainted with two men who needed the Saviour. "How long will we be gone?"

"A couple of days."

That meant taking along grub enough for at least a week. Ray had learned that from the Indians who frequently went out on the big lake.

They left Camsell Portage early the next morning, a bright fall day with a few scattered clouds breaking the blue of the sky. There was a little wind kicking shallow wavelets across the smooth lake as they nosed out from the dock, the motor slicing the heavily loaded canoe through the icy blue water. Two hours from shore Norman Chopping eyed the horizon. An almost imperceptible change had taken place. The clouds in the distance were ominously dark and close together and the swells were deepening.

"Wind's coming up, Ray," he said cryptically.

The missionary nodded.

Here and there a thin, lacy edge of white appeared on the crest of a wave.

"Will we turn and run for it?"

He shook his head. "It's too late for that now." Expertly he angled the craft into the deepening swells and cut the speed. "There's an island out here somewhere. If we can make it, we'll hole up until this blow's over."

The waves built steadily as the velocity of the wind increased, taxing the skill of the man at the motor. One after another, the breakers slid under the big canoe. She lifted on the huge seas, poised for an instant on the crest and plunged sluggishly into the trough behind. For the space of a heartbeat she wallowed there while water towered above them in all directions. Then she began to lift again.

Slowly time dragged by. At reduced speed the canoe seemed to crawl painfully over the waves; lifting and plunging over breakers that seemed determined to swamp them. In spite of Norman's skill with the boat, water poured over the side now and again. Ray and the other trapper were kept busy, bailing. The eight dogs that were to make up the trappers' dog team cowered motionless in the bottom of the canoe. They seemed to sense the danger.

The narrow finger of land appeared on the horizon and the trapper angled towards it. The change in direction, though slight, caused the canoe to pitch dangerously and threaten to yaw as the powerful waves slammed against her bow.

Their clothes were wet from the icy spray and the savage wind drove the cold to the marrow of their bones. Shivering, Ray paused in his bailing and looked for the island that seemed but little closer to them than it had an hour before.

For a time courage failed him.

'Was this why God had brought him to Lake Athabasca?' he wondered. 'Was this to be the end of his service for the Master?'

Grimly he shook away the fear.

They were getting closer to the island. That was sure. He could make out the contour of the island, could see that it had been burned over recently and there was little vegetation of any kind on it. The canoe continued to creep forward until, at last, they were ashore. Unloading their gear, they pulled the canoe far out of the water, beyond the high water mark of the waves on the beach.

"We made it!" Norman grinned, shouting exultantly above the roar of the wind and the savage pounding of the waves against the rocks. "We made it!"

"We can praise God for that!" the missionary told him.

Already the two trappers were scouting the burned-over area for wood to build a fire. Ray Bradford joined them. On the lee side of the island they located a spot that was as sheltered from the wind as possible and built a fire. The warmth of the friendly flames began to lick the numbness from their exhausted bodies and they suddenly realized that they hadn't eaten since they left Camsell early that morning.

"It's a good thing we brought some extra food along," Ray said.

The trappers, experienced though they were in the North, looked at one another sheepishly. They had only brought a few sandwiches.

"We didn't think it was going to storm," Norman explained.

The storm lasted for three days and three nights. All that time leaving the island would have been foolhardy. With three men and eight dogs to feed Ray's little supply of food was soon gone. And for the last day and a half they had only coffee to dull their hunger.

The fourth morning when they got up the big lake had gone back to sleep again and the sun shone benignly from a cloudless sky. Striking across the calm lake they found an empty trapper's cabin with a bit of flour, salt and a little lard in the cupboard. They mixed the flour with water, added a little salt and fried it.

"I've never sat down to a banquet that tasted half so good," Ray said, "we were that hungry."

The years the Bradfords spent at Camsell Portage were filled with hardships and disappointments, as are the early years in almost any new field in the North. But there were rewards, too.

One young prospector spent a great deal of time with the missionary couple. That in itself was strange, for he was a Godless young white man with a vile tongue and an even more vile life. He and Ray spent a great deal of time in the bush together. Now and then the missionary got an opportunity to talk to him about the Saviour, but for the most part all he could do was live a Christian life before him. In all the time the two men were together there was no indication that anything had ever made an impression on him. Yet, on one occasion, he confided in a neighbor of the missionary couple.

"My," he said, his voice wistful. "I just wish I could live the way Mr. Bradford does. If I ever change my life it will be because of his testimony."

Then there was the elderly prospector who had come up to Camsell Portage from the States many years before and had been poking around the rocks along Lake Athabasca ever since.

For some reason he took quite an interest in the Bradfords when they came to the settlement. During those early months they visited him often, not only for advice and help, but in an effort to introduce him to the Saviour.

"I am a Christian," he surprised them by saying one day. "When I was a kid back in my home town the Salvation Army got hold of me and led me to the Lord." Then, reading the astonishment in their eyes, he laughed mirthlessly. "But I guess you'd never know it by the way I've lived. Knockin' around the way I have all these years, I've committed more sins than you prob'ly heard of."

He didn't come back to the Lord that evening, but the time did arrive when he repented of his sins and came back into fellowship with Christ. From that day on, whenever the Indians came to his shack, which was often because they liked and respected him, he would read a portion of the Bible to them.

"I ain't much on talkin', Ray," he would say, "but I can read to 'em."

The old man died suddenly at the age of 82 and Ray Bradford had the funeral service. Practically every Indian in the village was there.

"It was a wonderful opportunity to present the gospel of Christ," the missionary said later, "and to show what the Lord can do in a life. I'm positive the seed that was sown that afternoon will in time bring forth fruit to the glory of the Saviour."

Chapter 7

The big Norwegian from La Ronge.

From the very beginning of the work among the Indians the ties of the NCEM with the Canadian Sunday School Mission had been very close. Nils Folkvord, the burly Norwegian, who was a figure in the La Ronge area for 20 years or more, was first a CSSM missionary when the general superintendent asked him if he was interested in going north to open a new work.

La Ronge was just a place on the map to him, but it seemed to be the place where he was to go. So he set out, not quite sure how he would get there, or what he would do after he did.

In those days a person worked out one step of a trip at a time. Nils bought a train ticket to the end of the line. At Prince Albert he made inquiry and learned that he could get as far north as Montreal Lake by transport truck. That was still 45 miles from his destination, but it was in the right direction. Another passenger on the truck lived at La Ronge and had driven a team and wagon to Montreal Lake when he went out.

"You can go back with me if you want to," he offered.

"If I want to?" Folkvord echoed, the accent thick in his voice. "My friend, you are an answer to prayer."

It took them three days to make the last forty-five miles by team and wagon. Nobody had thought about building bridges in those days, but the missionary's new friend knew the river well. He went up stream to a shallow stretch and drove his team across it.

The area looked like an excellent site for a mission station, but by this time Folkvord was almost out of money. After a two weeks' visit, he went out to work in the harvest fields so he could buy the supplies he needed. Fall found him back in the cabin the Mission had rented for him.

The big Norwegian, towering over the shorter, more slender Crees, could be seen at almost any hour of the day, striding up and down the paths in the settlement, or out to one of the outlying cabins. Regular services weren't practical so early in the work there, but he could, and did, visit endlessly.

Instinctively, the Indians knew they had a friend in him and often came to visit him. With care he passed out his precious tracts. And his flannel board was always ready to give a lesson. Even the adults found them intriguing.

The year 1946 rolled around, and with it the Canadian Sunday School Mission decision to turn its Indian work over to the NCEM. That made no difference to Folkvord. He was much too busy to take more than passing notice. The new group was concerned about the Indian people. That was enough for him.

But he was lonely. There was a girl waiting for him back home. She had been waiting a long while, and so had he.

"I knew first hand what the Scriptures meant when they say, 'it was not good for man to be alone.' " he said. "So I undertook to remedy the situation."

He went south for the wedding and, after a brief honeymoon, left her with her parents and returned to La Ronge to get a cabin built for them to live in. The shack he had been using was no longer available. John Unger (now a veteran missionary who produces the Cree radio program) was with him to help with the construction. While they worked they lived in a tent and ate their meals outside.

"It wasn't exactly a mansion we were building," Folkvord said, blue eyes dancing. "It was 10 by 16 feet, built of rough lumber, and we didn't even have the ceilings in when I wired her that the place was finished and she should come."

Once when he was telling another missionary about it, he mentioned that the cabin was unfinished and that the only furniture they had was what he and John had nailed together. Surprise crossed the other man's face.

"And she stayed?" he asked incredulously.

Mrs. Folkvord had the answer for him.

"You couldn't have dragged me away," she said.

*   *   *

Someone had given Folkvord a fairly large tent, too old and tattered to be used on the windy prairies. Once the house was completed he and John Unger put up the tent and began having meetings three or four times a week. John played the guitar and sang and the big Norwegian brought the messages.

It was to those meetings that Gilbert came. His home was 20 miles north of La Ronge, but every summer he would bring his family down to the settlement, pitch his tent, and stay for several weeks. He began to come to the services, sitting in the same place on the same bench night after night. Folkvord saw that he was interested, but did not press the subject with him, personally.

One evening the missionary approached Gilbert after the service and invited him for a cup of tea. They had not been in the house long when Gilbert spoke up suddenly. "Is it a sin to play cards?"

Surprise glinted in Folkvord's eyes, but he did not let on.

"Now that you've asked me, Gilbert, I'll tell you my own experience. Before I became a Christian I used to play cards, but when I was saved I quit all those things."

There was a brief hesitation.

"Saved?" he echoed. "That's what I am."

"That's interesting, Gilbert. When did you get saved?"

"Down there in the tent."

*   *   *

While there are, and always have been sad cases of falling away among the Indian converts, Gilbert is not among them.

"I've watched him for years," Folkvord related. "It's been interesting to see him grow in the Lord."

On one occasion the missionary asked him if he would give his testimony at the next service. He hesitated briefly.

"I don't think I can," he replied. "My heart can never stand."

Gilbert continued to smoke for some time after he was saved. The missionary knew of it, but did not make an issue of his smoking. Instead he waited for the Lord to speak to him about it. Several years later the missionary was visiting him in his home on the Sucker River when the Indian spoke to him about it.

"Nils," he said suddenly, "I quit smoking."

"That's fine," Folkvord replied. "When did you do that?"

"About a year ago. I got to thinking about the other Christians I knew who didn't smoke. Then I remembered that the Bible tells us we should not love the world or the things of the world. So I took my cigarettes out of my pocket and laid them in the window. I haven't touched them since."

It wasn't long until Gilbert went to the Indian Bible School and graduated from the four year course.

"Now," the big Norwegian concluded, "Gilbert often brings

a ten minute message at our evening services. I'm glad to say that his heart can stand it. And what is more important, his life measures up to what he says so his words carry weight with his fellow Indians who hear him."

*   *   *

Every spring the difficult task of cutting the season's firewood begins. Trees are cut down, sawed and split to dry for the coming winter's use. It is a big enough task on any station, but particularly so at Montreal Lake where the school, the dormitories and the homes of the teachers and workers must be heated with wood.

Folkvord went down to Montreal Lake that spring of 1960 to help them cut wood. The big Norwegian had spent years in the woods and could do the work of two ordinary men.

The big Norwegian had spent years in the woods.

"Put Nils on one end of a 'Swede saw' " one of the missionaries said, "and he'd have you panting trying to handle the other end before you got more than a couple of trees cut up."

The first hours of this particular morning he had spent splitting wood, but after a break for coffee he took up one of the power saws and started felling trees. Even though he handled the big crosscuts with ease he was glad for the power saws that speeded up the work, even for him.

They had not been working long when he dropped a big jack pine. It fell in the direction he intended it to fall, but brushed against a dead tree as it went down. The towering, naked trunk swayed forward under the glancing blow, came back in a pendulum arc, and broke off about twenty feet from the top. The top crashed to the ground, striking Nils Folkvord on the back of the head.

"I looked around quickly," John Penner, who was with him at the time wrote, "but at first I couldn't see him. The blow had knocked him to the ground."

By the time he got over to where Folkvord was lying the stunned man had regained consciousness and was staring blankly up at his friend.

"What was it?" he asked brokenly. "What happened?"

"Your tree brushed a dead one." Tenderly John reached out and touched Folkvord's badly injured head. "Are you all right? Do you hurt anywhere?"

Nils nodded, closing his eyes and clenching his fists against the savage, relentless waves of pain that swept over him. He had felt pain before, had shrugged it off, ignored it. But never had he felt pain like this. It started in the back of his head where the tree struck him and surged through his body in a mighty crescendo.

He began to pray, first in Norwegian, and then in English, hopelessly tangling the two languages in his agony.

"Dear God, take care of my dear wife and children," he pleaded. "Undertake for them and ease their concern and . . . and . . ." The words choked off as great surging blows of pain slammed through his tortured body. "The pain is more than I can stand, Lord," he murmured, "take me home!"

But his friend, listening, was praying in another way.

"Lord, don't let him go! Not here in the bush!"

Penner ran to get help from others who were cutting wood not far away. One of the group ran home for the stretcher and somebody else brought a car to the nearest spot on the road.

When they carried him out it looked as though they were already too late. He was foaming at the mouth and only the whites of his eyes showed. Mercifully, he had lost consciousness.

"Do you think he'll live?" somebody asked.

His missionary friend choked and looked away.

At Montreal Lake they stopped only long enough to have the Hudson Bay manager radio Prince Albert for an ambulance to start north to meet them. Then they drove on as fast as possible under the existing road conditions. Forty miles out of Prince Albert they met the ambulance and transferred him to it for the remainder of the trip.

After the first examination the doctors were guardedly optimistic.

"Conditions look fair for his survival," they said after a preliminary examination, "unless complications set in."

That night there were serious complications. And by morning he had been rushed to Saskatoon where he lay in a deep coma for ten days.

"There's very little hope for him," the specialist in Saskatoon said. "His chances are slim."

But he was reckoning without the intervention of a prayer-answering God. For six or seven weeks Nils Folkvord lay unconscious on his hospital bed while missionaries and interested friends across Canada and the United States prayed. Once he regained consciousness, he spent a like period in the hospital rebuilding his strength.

His speech was affected for months and his sense of balance was so impaired that he walked with crutches for a year, and was never able to walk again without the use of a cane.

*   *   *

When Nils Folkvord recovered from the injury that bothered him for so long it would have seemed that God had a long and fruitful ministry for him. Such was not the case, however.

In the summer of 1965 he had word that the McPherson family were arriving in Prince Albert from Fort Churchill on their way to the Bible school at La Ronge. Nils drove to Prince Albert, picked up the McPherson family (there were six or seven) and started back. Late in the evening he drove over a hill near La Ronge. The wind had died and the dust hung on the road in great opaque clouds. Approaching the crest of the hill he met another car, which added to the smoke screen he had to drive through. The dust was so thick Nils never did see the car he hit head-on.

Folkvord was killed almost instantly.

Herb McPherson was taken to the hospital in Prince Albert with a broken leg and one of the children was injured.

*   *   *

Stan Williams is one of the former students who remains as a living monument to Mr. Folkvord's ministry in La Ronge. He drove in to La Ronge with his family of five in an old car to prepare himself to preach the gospel, having left a good job to come.

Stan graduated from the Bible school and today is ministering among his own people and has a radio broadcast.

"He is doing a very good work for the Lord," Folkvord once reported. "But, as I tell folks, 'if God can save a Norwegian, He can save an Indian. And if He can save them, He can make evangelists of them.' "

Chapter 8

Africa was their chosen field.

Many areas of the North have proved to be difficult, almost impossible places for a missionary to work. Drunkeness, immorality, gambling and all the forces of darkness seem to present a solid front against the gospel. Should a single individual give evidence of weakening, the entire community will unite against him, blasting him with persecution and scorn until, all too often, he lapses back into the old life.

La Loche, Saskatchewan is such a place.

Missionaries had been working there since shortly after the NCEM was founded, but without visible results. Two single girls went in first, followed by a couple who had to leave because of illness (the wife had contracted tuberculosis, the scourge of the Indians and that area in particular). And so the Wellwoods were sent there.

Africa was their chosen field of service. They had finished their preparation, had taken a language course, and were seeking acceptance ready to leave. But God had other plans for them. He wanted them on their own side of the ocean in a place as hard and unfruitful as any community of Africa could be.

They had waited two years to go to the dark continent. Two months after receiving a letter from Stan Collie they had been accepted and were on the field at La Loche, strong evidence to them that they were in the centre of the Lord's will.

In the years that followed they were to need that assurance again and again, the way seemed so hard, the field so unfruitful.

Robby Fontaine was on the plane that took the Wellwoods in. The name meant little outside the area, but he was an important Chipewyan, very likely the best known individual in the entire village. He seemed to like the missionaries and became the most consistent visitor in the Wellwood home.

But even the friendship of so important a personage was not enough to allay the fears of the people, nor did it lessen the opposition. At first the Wellwoods tried to do visitation and hold Bible studies in the homes. But they soon discovered the people were afraid they might have visitors who would spread the word that they allowed the preacher to come into their home and read the Bible.

Next they tried to hold Sunday school. There was excellent response to Sunday school at first and the youngsters, interested, began to drop in to the Wellwood home after supper to sing. They loved the simple gospel melodies, and every night for a week or so they showed up. Their numbers increased until 18 or 20 were coming and the missionaries were beginning to get encouraged.

"Maybe La Loche isn't going to be as hard for us as it was for the others," Wellwood said.

Then, without warning, persecution started and attendance dropped.

"Do you suppose it's something we've said or done, Dorothy?" he asked, concern darkening his eyes.

She shook her head.

"I think they've been given orders to stay away from here and not have anything to do with us," she said.

It was two or three months before any of the children dared to be friendly to them again.

Wellwood and his wife found the people friendly, but there was fear in their eyes, fear planted by others who were determined that the new missionaries should not reach anyone for Christ.

"They are dangerous!" the Indians were told. "They will take your souls to hell if they can. The only safe thing for you and your children is to leave them alone."

But there was great need among them. And on occasion, their need overruled their fear. There were times when, for two or three days, entire families would only have a little meat or fish to eat. When the time for the mail plane approached and they were going to have checks coming for furs or fish, the Wellwoods could be sure they would have callers.

"We have nothing at our house," the man would say. "Could

I borrow a little lard, some flour, sugar and baking powder? About a dollar's worth, maybe?"

"We soon learned that it was usually safe to advance them a little food. Seldom would an Indian fail to pay a food bill."

On the other hand, the Wellwoods discovered all too painfully, that they could not lend them anything else. They were inveterate gamblers. In the spring when money was plentiful from furs and fish gambling was rampant.

"One poker game lasted more than 36 hours without stopping," Wellwood reported. "It only ended when so many were broke that there was no one to keep playing."

The same people who came to borrow food refused to work for Wellwood more than a day or two, although he needed their help desperately to get in his wood and to put up hay for his cow.

"That situation began to change a little as we became better acquainted," he said. "But it continued in varying degrees all the time we were there."

By getting one man for a couple of days, and then another, and by befriending all of them and helping them as much as he could, he was able to get his work done and come to be considered as their friend. Yet, he was not able to preach to more than a few at a time.

They seemed friendly enough but only five or six would come out for a service. Distrust darkened many eyes and sealed many pairs of lips.

"We were able to get close enough to some of them," he said, "that they trusted us implicitly."

And it seemed that they were loved by the people, but their fear of censure was too great to permit them to become very open and friendly.

Then the thing happened which apparently had been God's purpose for sending the Wellwoods to La Loche. As he sent Philip from Jerusalem to Gaza so he could meet the Ethiopian on the way, it seemed that He sent the Wellwoods to La Loche, to meet Tommy and Helen Francis.

Tommy had left one of the Cree reservations as a young man, joined the Air Force and served until the end of World War II. Upon his release he applied to the Department of Natural Resources, went to school two winters, served a year at Cumberland House, and was assigned to La Loche.

Although of unusual ability and ambition, Tommy was well on his way to alcohol addiction. But he was friendly and he and Helen began to attend the Wellwoods' Sunday services.

The Hudson Bay manager and his wife seemed interested too, and came regularly until they were transferred a short time later. The Wellwoods wondered whether Tommy and Helen would continue to attend after the Bay manager and his wife left. But they did. About six months after attending the first service Helen Francis made her decision for Christ.

"What rejoicing there was in our home that night!" Wellwood said exultantly. "We had our first sister in Christ among our Indian people."

In the spring, about a year after he first came to La Loche, Tommy Francis was out in the bush fighting fire with a group of Indians.

"Tommy," one of them said, "you've got a different belief than ours. Just what is it that you believe, anyway?"

"Well for one thing," he began slowly, "We believe that a person can't work his way to Heaven. He's got to see that he's a sinner and is going to hell unless he does something about it. And . . . . And the only thing he can do that will really help him is to confess his sin and put his trust in Christ to save him . . . ."

Tommy Francis continued to talk. His listeners were just curious, but each word he said burned its way into his own heart. This was what he had been hearing Sunday after Sunday, it was true. But he had never made it a reality in his heart. He had never done what he was telling those men that he believed. He had never confessed his sin and asked the Lord Jesus Christ to save him.

As he sat with his men on the fire line he yielded his heart to Christ.

There were a few others who made a profession of faith during the Wellwoods' stay at La Loche. Several made decisions just before they died. Even the deaths of those new believers were a testimony as the relatives and neighbors gathered around.

"He died happy," they would say in awe.

But there were disappointments and failures, too. Some of the converts could not stand the persecution and fell away. One young man went through the motions of a decision when he was desperately ill, only to forget about it when he got back on his feet.

Although the Wellwoods spent a total of eight years at La Loche, Tommy and Helen Francis appeared to be the only living converts who were standing true.

The Lord took Tommy out of the Department of Natural Resources. He and Helen went down to Cass Lake, Minnesota to the Christian and Missionary Alliance Indian Bible School. Upon graduation he returned to serve the NCEM as an Indian evangelist and Bible teacher to his own people. The lives of Tommy and his wife are unimpeachable testimonies to the Indian people who know and respect and love him.

Fly with a missionary almost anywhere in the North and you are likely to be approached by someone who knows him.

"Tommy Francis has been in here to speak," they say. Or, "Tell Tommy hello when you see him. He's a friend of mine."

Wellwood has found the dedicated evangelist and his wife to be a constant encouragement.

"Whenever I think the going's so slow that we're wasting our time," he said, "I remember Tommy and Helen. We were eight years in La Loche and they were the only lasting results. Yet we can take real strength from the knowledge that through Tommy and Helen hundreds of their own people have been won for the Saviour."

When the Wellwoods moved to the Maritimes to open a new work there Tommy was able to help them in a very practical way. He and his family journeyed east to the Maritimes where he went with the veteran missionary doing personal work and giving his testimony when it seemed advisable.

It was the men who came to hear the Indian preacher from the prairies. Young and middle aged men listened avidly while he told them of being delivered from the clutches of alcohol. Although there were no souls saved on that trip there was great interest.

At one place three brothers were home. They defended the way they believed as Tommy and Wellwood sought to present the Lord Jesus Christ to them. One of the boys surprised his brothers by siding in with the missionaries.

"Now wait a minute!" the oldest exclaimed peevishly. "You're supposed to be on my side. Just whose side are you on, anyway."

A year later the Wellwoods stopped to see an elderly woman on the same reserve.

"God must be trying to punish me," she said miserably. "I've got three drunkards for sons."

"God won't punish you for the sins of your sons," the missionary had the joy of telling her. "He punished His Son for your sin." He went on to explain the way of Salvation.

Before they left she asked him to pray for her and for her three boys.

"We'll do that," he said, "and ask some of our friends to pray for you, too. But before we go, let's pray now."

There, standing in the middle of the living room floor they

bowed their heads and he asked God to bless her, to save her soul
and to give her the peace that Jesus Christ came to give her.

When they finished praying she said, "My, that is such a relief.
It seemed like my heart opened up and my troubles went out while
you were praying."

Joseph Paul was one of the converts of the Wellwoods in the
Maritime Provinces. But, let Joseph tell about it himself.

"My name is Joseph Paul. I live at St. Mary's Indian Reserve
in Fredericton, New Brunswick. I used to go out and drink and
gamble and all the things that are against our Lord. I had been
doing that for years.

"One day I am over in State of Main picking potatoes. I see
Eddie Bear one evening and we are talking.

" 'A missionary was down to my place,' he said.

"I say to myself, this is great opportunity for me. I should try
to get the missionary to come and see me.

" 'Send him down where I live,' I tell Eddie. 'I like to see him.'

" 'Yeah, I'll send him over,' he says.

"I did not think he come so soon, but that next evening he is
there and introduce himself to me. 'I am Art Wellwood,' he tell me.

"And he took his Bible and start teaching me. I know right
then that this was the thing I was looking for. Deep in my heart I
know this is what I want . . . . Somebody to teach me of God. I
needed the Lord.

"But I can say nothing then until three or four nights after
teaching from the Bible by Art. Then one night I accept the Lord
as my personal Saviour. From that moment on my life seemed to
change.

"After that I was glad to talk about my Lord to anyone I met,
especially to my own people—Indian. When I got home I told my
wife and family that I was saved. Finally all my family got saved.
It was a great day for us. It was a great day for every one of us
in our family to be saved. Like Paul, one day, we are working for
something that will last forever. That is Eternal Life we have with
the Lord. Amen."

Chapter 9

I listen to your Cree Broadcast.

Ada Arcand had her religion. She had been born to it, even as she had been born a Cree. It was a part of her way of life, a form to be followed, however infrequently. To be sure, there were times when she was disturbed by her religion. It didn't satisfy the inner longings of her heart. It didn't remove the love for liquor or tobacco or the things of the world that meant so much to both her husband, Albert, and herself. Their lives were little different than they would have been had they remained as pagan as their ancestors.

All that religion did for her was to provide an uncertain insulation against the harsh realities of death. It engendered a faint hope that somehow she would be found worthy of heaven.

She was entirely unprepared for what she heard the day she first chanced upon the Back to the Bible Broadcast. The words seared her soul.

Sin had to be faced by each individual, personally. 'All have sinned and come short of the glory of God.' 'There is none righteous. No, not one.'

There was hope in that first message, but she didn't hear it. The reality of sin—her own sin—drummed too loudly in her ears.

Her first reaction was to snap off the radio and force such disturbing thoughts from her mind. But she could not. They would not be stilled so easily. And the next morning at the same time she listened again, eagerly. The next day she listened, and the next,

59

and the next. Soon she found that by flipping the dial she could
find it on another station at another time.

The weight of sin did not leave her as she listened, but something else was added, something that brought a note of joy. God
so loved her and her husband that He provided a way of escape.
It did not change the indictment of death that hung over each
person because of sin. It provided payment for that sin, the death
of the Lord Jesus Christ on the Cross.

That had happened for her! Ada Arcand!

Before the radio in their little cabin she accepted Christ as
her Saviour. By this time she had discovered that their radio would
pick up six different stations that carried the Back to the Bible
Broadcast. And she was listening to it six times a day, avidly
clinging to every word.

Her concern for her family came almost immediately.

"Albert," she would say, "listen to the Broadcast with me."
He listened, but found it difficult to understand.

"Don't you see how it is?" she asked him. "You have to

"Albert, listen to the broadcast with me."

confess your sin and accept Jesus Christ as your Saviour in order to go to heaven."

His forehead wrinkled.

"I don't understand English as good as you, Ada," he told her.

Her concern for Albert grew. She tried to explain to him. He tried to understand. But it seemed hopeless. She lacked a knowledge of the Scriptures and his cautious mind was filled with unanswered questions.

Then she discovered a broadcast in the Cree language over the Prince Albert station. She didn't know that it had originated in Meadow Lake a few weeks before as an extension of the ministry of the NCEM. She didn't even know the Northern Canada Evangelical Mission existed. But as she listened to the simple fifteen minute program her heart thrilled. This was the same message the Back to the Bible Broadcast preached only it was in Cree. Her fingers trembled as she jotted down the time and station.

The next time it came on she made sure that Albert was there to hear it.

"Now you can understand," she said confidently.

Albert listened to that broadcast but made no comment. The next week he heard it, and the next, and the next. He listened carefully enough and would talk with Ada about the message when it was over.

"Yes," he said with characteristic slowness of speech. "I can understand it better in Cree. He makes plain the things he says. But——"

That was the stone wall Ada could not get him through. Doubt and hesitation mingled with the questions in his mind.

She was praying for Albert one day when the thought came to her. The man who did the speaking on the Cree program did not live so far away. (By this time she had learned that the program was transcribed in Meadow Lake.) Maybe he would come and talk to Albert personally. Maybe——if he really was concerned about the Indian people he preached to—he would drive the 100 miles or more to Canwood and help answer her husband's questions.

The letter was written and sent prayerfully.

"Dear Sir:

"My husband and I listen to your Cree Broadcast regularly. Would you please come over and talk to Albert about Jesus? He finds it so hard to understand.

Sincerely,
Ada Arcand"

The letter went to John Unger who had been responsible for setting up the Cree portion of the Indian Gospel Broadcast. It would have been easy for him to rationalize the letter away.

There was no knowing whether Albert even wanted to talk to anyone about the Saviour. His wife had been the one to write. It was the middle of the winter and a 200 mile trip in his old car with the tires as poor as they were was no small undertaking. Besides, he had many demands on his time—work that was crying to be done.

Still, there was sincerity in Ada's letter and a note of quiet desperation. If he didn't go, who was there to help them?

So he made the trip to Canwood and found Albert Arcand eager to talk with him. He was able to answer the unsaved man's questions and Albert became a Christian. Ada's prayers were answered.

The Indian Gospel Broadcast has been answering the prayers of both missionaries and Christian Indians since its inauguration in the fall of 1957.

According to one veteran member of the Board, Stan Collie regularly mentioned the need for such a program at various meetings of the Board. Just as regularly, they would all agree with him.

"Yes, it would be a fine thing. Who's going to do it?"

With that the suggestion would die for another year.

Then John Unger was suggested. He had learned Cree exceptionally well, and Cree, the language of one of the largest tribes in the North, was the logical one with which to begin.

As so often happens in the launching of something new, the Mission was not long in discovering that the ministry of the radio program was far greater than they had even dared to hope for. It not only brought the gospel to the Indian people in their own language, it opened doors for personal work by the missionaries and served as an introduction to the Cree Witness, the monthly publication in that language.

"When I do house to house visitation in a village where I'm not known," a missionary said, "I always introduce myself as being a part of the group that has the Cree Broadcast and ask if they listen to it."

Even in homes that are hostile to the gospel and to the missionaries the program is regularly listened to.

In one such instance Unger was making calls on a certain Indian reservation when he was met at the door of one home by an icy stare.

"We've been warned by our minister about letting anyone

else in to talk to us or have a service," she said. "You're not wanted here. There's no reason for you to come in."

"I won't preach to you or try to hold a service if you don't want me to," he assured her. "But I would like to come in and visit for a few minutes, if you don't mind."

She stepped aside and allowed him to enter. The house was fairly large and there were a number of people there. He talked with them for a few minutes and then identified himself.

"I'm with the group that has the Indian Gospel Broadcast." Her eyes lighted.

"You do!" she exclaimed, her entire manner changing. "Think of that! We listen all the time!" She paused. "In that case you can have a service here, if you'd like."

Unger opened his Cree New Testament, read to them from it and explained the gospel to them. They sang and had prayer.

When he rose to leave the same Indian woman followed him to the door and took his hand gratefully.

"I'm so glad you came. I appreciate the passage you read from the Bible."

In northern Manitoba Collie and Unger flew into an isolated settlement where the people were very poor. As soon as they landed one of the men said, "there is no fishing or hunting. We have no grub."

Before the missionaries left they went into one of the homes for a short service. Unger noticed a radio speaker fastened to the wall of the drafty little cabin.

"And what is that for?" he asked.

"My radio broke," the Indian said. "We put that in and fasten to Joe's radio in next cabin. Now we can listen to the Cree Broadcast, too."

Letters come in too, unsolicited, that give a glimpse of the accomplishments of the short weekly broadcast.

Unger first heard from Albert Snake by mail. The aged Indian spoke only Cree and had never heard the gospel before the broadcast in his native tongue came on.

"Dear Sir:

"Every Saturday I am sure glad to hear you over the radio. You said over the radio that if anyone wants a calendar he's got to write to you. I am sending best regards to you all. Me, Albert Snake. Best of luck to you all and may God bless you all night and day."

That letter came in 1959. Unger had occasion to visit with

him and talk with him about the Saviour, as well as by correspondence. Then, in December, 1963 a letter came from Albert's son.

"Dear Friend:

"Writing a short letter to you to let you know that we are all fine. At present time the Lord has been good to us, and I thank the Lord for that.

"But I am sorry to tell you that my dad passed way. Maybe you heard about it already. Yes, I know that our Lord took him to heaven. He didn't have any suffering and no pain. He just like going to sleep. Jesus close his eyes, and I thank Jesus for that He took my dad. I know my dad is happy now.

"He used to listen to you every Saturday 5 o'clock over Prince Albert CKBI and we still do the same. Please send me the Cree Witness and calendar. May God bless you all, and your family, and keep you in good health. Merry Christmas and a Happy New Year to you all.

Yours friend,

Alfred Snake."

The Cree broadcast proved to be so successful that a program in the Chipewyan language was launched. Veteran missionary Bud Elford prepares the tapes in that language. Although the Chipewyan tribe is much smaller than the Cree, the broadcasts in that language have been most successful.

As well, the NCEM is responsible for an Ojibway program in Ontario. Mr. Stan Williams, an Ojibway Indian and a former La Ronge Indian Bible School student is the speaker.

There is no glamour involved in preparing a message and a fifteen minute program in an Indian language every week. There is no excitement in preparing tapes and in answering the few letters that come in, or in making personal visits for followup. The work of the missionaries actually serving on stations may seem more intriguing. Yet the Indian Gospel Broadcast is making an impact on Godless hearts that could not be reached in any other way. It is the strong right arm of the missionary effort of the NCEM.

Chapter 10

We could build our own furniture.

Shortly after breakfast the day before the first printing press was to arrive at Buffalo Narrows for the Mission Stan Collie looked at his watch.

"Well, I guess I'd better get going. The truck is to be at Fort Black tomorrow morning."

"Want me to go along?" Tarry asked.

"It's only what they call an 8 by 12. It can't be very big. But if you want to go along it's fine with me."

That was in the fall of 1946. The newly organized mission had found that they needed a printing press to get out literature acquainting Christian friends with the work they were doing. So someone had purchased a used press for them in Winnipeg. It had gone to Meadow Lake by rail and up the tortuous trail north to Fort Black by transport truck at a laborious 5 miles an hour.

The fact that nobody at the mission had operated a press disturbed neither Collie or Tarry as they made their way south to the place where they were to meet the truck. After all, they cut wood, fixed their outboard motors, and tinkered with their radios and anything else that needed fixing. All a press did was put words on paper. There couldn't be anything so complicated about that.

And so they were waiting with their scow when the truck groaned to a stop.

"You the guys for the printing press?" the driver asked wearily.

"That's right."

"O.K. I'll back down into the water as far as I can to help you load it."

Collie looked at him.

"Is that necessary?"

The burly trucker returned the gaze.

"It is unless you're a lot stronger than I think you are."

The missionaries' eyes widened as the big truck inched back into the water.

"There must be some mistake," Art Tarry said uneasily. "That big crate couldn't possibly be for us."

"You're from the NCEM, whatever that is, ain't you?" the truck driver asked when they questioned him a moment or two later.

Stan Collie nodded.

"Then this is for you. One printing press. That's what it says on my bill. And that's what's in the box." He unfastened the tailgate. "Now help me get this thing off, will you? I've got to get on my way."

Sweat soaked their shirts and their backs ached when finally they succeeded in scooting the heavy crate from the truck to the back of the scow. The trucker squinted at it and then in the direction of Buffalo Narrows.

"Good luck," he said cryptically. "And it looks to me as though you'll need it."

Precariously they made their way back fifty miles over lakes and rivers to Buffalo Narrows. A gang of men helped them get it onto the dock and up to Art Tarry's house.

"Now," Collie said, his dismay showing through, "what are we going to do with it?"

"We can't put it in the living room the way we planned," Tarry answered. "That's for sure."

So it was decided that they would place the press beside the house and build a room around it. This they did as soon as possible to protect it from the weather. At last the room was ready and they uncrated the press before the silent, wondering eyes of their families.

"Boy" one of the kids exclaimed in awe. "I never saw anything like that before."

"Neither have I," Tarry retorted, walking about it warily. "But how do you run it?"

Stan Collie shook his head.

"You've got me. But I can tell you this much, as heavy as it is, a fella could get killed with it if he did the wrong thing."

Due deliberation, however, revealed that it was operated by a foot pedal. Step down on it and the form was pressed against the paper, release the pressure and it came up.

"There's nothing so complicated about that," one of them observed.

Their confidence returned.

"Suppose we ought to try it, eh?"

"I'm game," Collie said. "What'll we print?"

"What I'm wondering," his fellow missionary countered, "is, where's the type?"

"I'd never thought of that. We will have to have type, won't we?"

They studied the cumbersome press once more.

"It's got to be around here somewhere. They surely wouldn't send out a machine without some type."

"Here we are," Tarry exclaimed, moments later, pulling out the square, box-like tympan. "I thought surely they'd——" His words choked off "There's no type in this thing."

At last they came to the realization that there was no type with the press and finally learned the name of a company in the East where they could order it. It was weeks later that a letter arrived saying they would soon be receiving the type they had ordered.

"Although you didn't order it," the letter said, "you will be needing a quantity of quoins and furniture (pieces of birch for spacing, etc.). We are sending them along with our compliments . . ."

"It's a good thing they're donating that furniture," Collie muttered as he read the letter. "If they weren't they'd sure hear from us. We could build our own furniture."

At last the type, quoins and furniture arrived and they were ready to go to work. Art's wife placed the various letters in little paper bags, and as each letter was needed the correct bag was sought.

As laboriously as they had loaded the press onto the scow they set up the first bit of type. John 3:16. That was the message to which the press was dedicated.

"It's all set," Tarry said at last.

Stan Collie pressed on the foot pedal and the old press began to roll. What it had printed before they did not know, but from now on it was to be used to the glory of God.

The missionary took the first copy in his hand and squinted at it.

"It's sort of blotched, isn't it?"

His partner couldn't help grinning.

"You've got so much ink on you, Stan, it's hard to tell whether the paper, or you, went through the press."

"Let me tell you something. You're not so clean yourself."

But with experience they began to learn how to operate the press.

It was four years later that Owen Salway and his wife came to Buffalo Narrows to take care of the printing. After the Mission moved its headquarters to Meadow Lake and modernized its printing Abe Heppner joined him.

*   *   *

"Good words," she said brokenly.

Miss Mary Edwards, instructor in the Cree language school in the mid 1950's was concerned about the lack of reading material in Cree. When a Cree syllabic typewriter was bought the way opened to bring out the CREE CHRISTIAN, the forerunner of the CREE WITNESS.

Those who didn't know English welcomed something they could read in their own language. Those who are struggling to learn

Cree, and there are many Indians in that category among the middle aged and younger people these days, find the little paper intriguing.

Like the Cree Broadcast it goes behind doors closed by fear, indifference and superstition. It finds ready acceptance among many who will not allow anyone to speak to them about the Lord Jesus Christ.

One aged Cree woman, her dark face lined by years of hardship and trouble, tapped the issue she had been reading.

"Good words," she said brokenly.

*   *   *

When Lorena Goosen first came to the mission she went through the language school at Meadow Lake taking the prescribed course in Cree. She did not give evidence of being especially gifted in that difficult language and there was no thought of using her on the CREE WITNESS. She went with one of the other single girls to do relief work in three Indian villages.

After a time a need developed in the Cree literature office.

"After praying about the matter we decided to ask Lorena if she would consider the job," Ray Bradford said. "It developed that she had a flair for writing and has done an excellent job."

The magazine in Cree has made a real impact wherever it has been distributed.

Chapter 11

I've flown everything else.

The float plane is the pack mule of the North; it is the magic carpet that picks up prospectors, trappers and missionaries alike and whisks them over deceptive miles of muskeg, rough water and roadless forests. It makes minutes of travel that used to take days, and opens up vast areas to the gospel that were all but closed because of difficult terrain.

Marshall Calverley well knew the advantage of a plane in the North when he went to Bible school with a view to becoming a missionary to the Indians. He had been a Hudson's Bay Company Fur Trader at Eastmain on the Quebec side of James Bay. He knew what it was to slog mile after mile behind a team of straining dogs in the 50 degrees below zero temperatures of December. He knew what it was to fight a canoe over mountainous waves in a desperate struggle to reach a sheltered cove or harbor. He and Erika knew all about isolation in their three years of married life on the Bay.

When he came to the Mission it was with a small plane which he had just learned to fly. With it he flew back into the very territory around Hudson Bay where he had worked for the Hudson's Bay Company, this time for a much more important employer, the Lord Jesus Christ.

"The tide was something of a problem at York Factory," he said. "If a pilot beached his plane at high tide it would be 50 yards from the water when the tide went out. If he beached it at low tide it wouldn't be long until it was floating again.

The Indians solved that problem for him.

When he came in twenty or so would crowd around the little craft, pick it up bodily and carry it beyond the reaches of the high tide. When he was ready to leave he would get in and they would reverse the process, carrying him out and depositing him in the water.

Marshall was soon to discover that the aircraft not only opened up territory for the missionary that had previously been too inaccessible to be practical, it provided many opportunities to witness that he had not anticipated.

On one occasion in midwinter he had flown from a place north of Winnipeg on his way home to Buffalo Narrows when the weather forced him down at Deschambault Lake. He landed at the mission station there and waited for the weather to clear.

It was an exasperating period.

The next morning it was clear at Deschambault but the weather at Buffalo Narrows was dirty.

"I'm sorry, old chap," the radio operator told him "We're socked in tight. Zero—zero. Even the snow birds are walking."

The next day it was snowing and blowing at Deschambault, and Buffalo Narrows reported beautiful weather. And so it went for an entire week. If conditions were such that he could get into the air, they were bad at his destination. If they were good at home, they were too rough for him to risk a take-off at Deschambault.

"There's a young fellow here I'd like to have you talk to," Art Acton, the missionary, said the first or second evening Marshall had been stranded there. "I've been trying to deal with him, and he seems interested, but I can't seem to answer all of his questions in a way that satisfies him."

"If you've talked to him I don't see any point in my seeing him," the flier countered. "I couldn't tell him anything you haven't already said."

The next afternoon Acton again asked him about going to see the Indian man.

"He was baptized as a child," his host persisted. "I think he's under conviction now, but that early baptism has got him all mixed up. He's got the idea that it makes him a Christian. I'd sure like to have you see him."

"Maybe I will," Marshall replied. Right at the moment he was much more concerned about the weather than he was in talking to a young Indian.

When he had been weathered in for almost a week the missionary's request became so insistent he could no longer ignore it.

"All right," he agreed with some reluctance. "I'll go and talk with him tomorrow morning. But I don't see that it can do any good."

The following morning he walked down to the little log cabin where Oscar Beatty, his wife and three small children lived.

Oscar was a likeable chap. He invited the missionary inside and listened patiently while Marshall showed him what the Bible had to say about baptism and how it related to salvation and faith.

When he finished the young Cree was as inscrutable as ever. There was no knowing whether anything that had been said had registered or not.

"That," Marshall said to himself as he trudged back through the snow, "was a waste of time. About all I did was satisfy our missionary."

The next morning the weather cleared and he was able to go on to Buffalo Narrows.

It was weeks later before he heard the end of the story. Oscar Beatty took his dog team and started out to his trap line shortly after Marshall's visit with him. He was pondering what the missionary said to him when, quite suddenly, it all became clear. On the trail beside his dogs he knelt, confessed his sin, and accepted Christ as his Saviour. When he got to his feet he took his tobacco from his pocket and heaved it into the bush.

Oscar returned from his trapping to show by his life that he was a changed man, and to witness to his people. He was reviled by his former friends, but that only made him stand the more firm. Although he was saved more than 12 years ago his testimony has been clear and unblemished and he has shown a real concern for the souls of his people.

"I don't know whether it was design or coincidence," Marshall recalled, "but the weather was bad until after I talked with Oscar. Then it cleared so I could take off. I've often wondered if I would have gotten out of there any sooner if I had seen him the first time, or how long God would have left me there if I had absolutely refused to go and talk to him."

At the same station a number of years later Marshall had flown one of the board members in for an inspection visit. The next morning an 18 year old lad we will call Joseph came down to the plane.

"I'd sure like to fly that thing," he said wistfully.

"You would, eh?" the pilot replied.

"I sure would. I'm going to learn to fly some day."

"Come on, I'll show you how the controls work."

They got into the 180 and for the next thirty minutes or so

talked planes and flying. Then Marshall broached the subject he
had been waiting for.

"There's something much more important for you than flying
a plane, Joseph," he started. And he began to tell him of the Lord
Jesus Christ who had died to pay the price of his sins.

Joseph was interested. He had been at the meeting the night
before and had been touched by something that had been said.
Some time before his dad had made a profession of faith and his
mother drove him out of the house. Still, his heart burned as the
missionary talked with him. Before they got out of the plane he
accepted Christ as his Saviour. And on the way back to the mission
station he glanced at Marshall.

"I sure do feel good!" he exclaimed.

When Joseph went home that morning and told what had
happened to him his older brother slapped his face. The persecution
the boy underwent was fierce.

This same brother took Joseph's Bible away from him, and
so-called friends got him drunk by taking him down and forcibly
pouring liquor down his throat. His mother was scornful and bitter.

It would be wonderful if one could write that he, too, had
been a rock in the trouble that came to him because of Christ.
Though he stood for a period and there seems to be no doubt
of his salvation, at the last report he wavered under the abuse and
was having a difficult time spiritually.

"It is easy to criticize a lad like that," Marshall said. "And,
frankly it is heartbreaking to have that happen to one who starts
out so well. But I often wonder how strong I would be if I had
to face what he and many of his fellow Indians have to face when
they take a stand for Christ."

*   *   *

Like all faith missions the NCEM has often felt a pinch from
lack of funds when there were projects crying for attention. In
1952 they bought a 5 place "Stinson Reliant" aircraft that had
been wrecked and Marshall was to rebuild it in Winnipeg. The work
took more than four months and cost more than five thousand
dollars.

"The plan was," he said, "to rebuild it as the Lord provided
the funds."

He was doing deputation as well as working on the plane, and
at times the progress on the plane ran ahead of the money available.

On one occasion he made arrangements for an electrician who
worked for Canadian Airlines to rewire the Stinson in his off hours.

"I'll do it for $150," he said.

"Fair enough."

"Only, when the job is finished I'll expect to be paid."

"That's fair enough, too," the missionary answered, although he didn't have fifteen dollars in his pocket at the time.

Marshall was at the airport late one afternoon when the fellow quit working for the day.

"I'll be finished tomorrow," he said. "There's not much left."

They both knew what he meant, and there was still no money to use to pay him.

On the way to town Marshall reached in his pocket and felt the gold ring he was carrying. It had quite a story.

It was the ring of a very old Winnipeg lady. When she heard him present the need for the plane in her church a few weeks before she came up and insisted that she give the ring to be sold and used on the plane.

"But I can't do that, Mrs. French," he protested. "This means a great deal to you."

"Now, Marshall," she exclaimed, "don't argue with me." She had known him since he was a kid. "I don't have very much time left on this earth and I want that ring to be of service to the Lord."

A couple of days later he went in to have the ring appraised.

"Actually," the jeweler said, "I would be stretching a point to give you $10.00 for it."

He shook his head.

"I think I'll keep it. The sacrifice of that dear old lady is worth a lot more than that."

Not long afterwards he was at the Winnipeg Bible Institute talking to a group of students and he pulled the ring from his pocket and told them the story. He had forgotten all about it. There had been more pressing things on his mind, like getting the electrician his $150.

The morning came when he was to pay the electrician. He had left the place he was staying and was driving out to the airport, pockets empty. He saw the matron of the Winnipeg Bible Institute walking towards the school so he stopped and gave her a ride.

"I'm glad you stopped, Marshall," she said, getting into the car. "I have something here I want to give you."

She handed him an envelope.

"I happened to overhear you tell some of the students about the old lady and her ring the other day," she went on. "I got to thinking about what she had done and that I had a car I actually didn't need."

So she had sold her car and was giving the proceeds to missions.

"Here's the part I want to go on your aircraft," she said, indicating the envelope she had handed him.

Marshall whipped over to the curb and stopped as soon as he got a couple of blocks down the street from the place where he let her out. In a general way she knew about the need for the plane, but she knew nothing about the pressing immediate need. His hands shook as he tore an end from the envelope and took out the check.

It was for exactly $150!

The electrician was paid on schedule.

*   *   *

The moment of take-off begins the most critical time in flight. The engine is practically wide open and the strain on controls, wing surfaces and fuselage is the greatest as the aircraft gains altitude. A look at the records will reveal that a large portion of crashes occur during that brief period.

Marshall Calverley was well acquainted with the hazards of take-off. By this time he had his commercial license with multi-engine and sea plane endorsements. In the flying he had done for the mission there had been periods of difficulty. They come to anyone who has spent considerable time in the air. There was an occasion when he had been forced down by carburetor icing, and another when he had engine failure in the air. Still another time, he had been flying an old war surplus twin engine plane in the Lake Athabasca area when a piston went through the cylinder, knocking out a motor. They had limped the rest of the way to Uranium City on one engine. All of those things had happened in flight, yet it was always the take-off that concerned him most.

Now he stood on the dock at Buffalo Narrows with the missionary he was going to fly to his station in an isolated area.

"I'll have to make a couple of trips," he said. "Is this all your gear?"

"Well——" the missionary was hesitant. "As a matter of fact I do have something else."

"Eh?"

"A billy goat."

Marshall's eyes widened. "A billy goat?"

"I've got a couple of goats," he explained. "We use the milk for the children." Concern flecked his voice. You can take him, can't you, Marshall?"

"I've flown everything else. I suppose I can take a billy goat."

The pilot took all he could on the first trip, came back and made ready to load the goat into the all-metal plane. As they tied the goat's legs Marshall laughed.

"Look at that guy's eyes. He's saying, 'if I could just get my horns into you'!"

At last the plane was loaded and ready for take-off. He taxied out into deep water, let the engine idle until the oil and engine temperature came up, and pushed open the throttle. The goat was heavy and the aircraft mushed along before coming up on the step. But at last the plane lifted into the air.

At that instant it happened.

"Bang!"

The plane jumped as though a bomb had gone off beneath it.

"My heart missed a couple of beats," Marshall related, "and my blood pressure shot up a hundred points! All I could think of was that a float had been torn off, or a section of a wing!"

But the aircraft continued to fly as though nothing had happened. Cautiously he eased back on the controls and it began to climb at a normal rate. Once he gained a little altitude he looked back.

"There was that old billy goat glaring at me! He had wriggled to one side and just as we left the water he had rammed the metal side of the plane with those heavy curved horns."

*   *   *

During the peak of the uranium fever at Uranium City on Lake Athabasca Marshall had another kind of a thrill. He had flown in as part of his job as mission pilot and had a layover for a week. While waiting he got acquainted with a prospector and agreed to fly him out to his camp a few miles from town. He spent most of the week with them. The next winter when he came back he learned that one of the fellows, his wife and baby had drowned.

What made it worse, Marshall had been with him for an entire week and hadn't once witnessed to him.

"Whether it was because there was no opportunity, or because I neglected to do so I'm not sure," he said. "But it bothered me terribly."

As soon as he could he looked up the partner who was still alive.

"Look, Cliff," he said bluntly. "Your friend that I met last summer is drowned. I'll never have a chance to talk with him again, or to preach the gospel to him. I don't even know whether I'll ever see you again. One or the other of us may be gone before this time next year. But I want to make sure that you know the way of salvation."

For two hours he talked with the prospector, his wife and their twelve year old daughter. The wife, it developed, was a Christian and had been praying for her husband for some time. He gambled considerably and probably drank as well. Most prospectors did. But that night he seriously considered the future for the first time in his life and made a decision for Christ.

He and his family joined the little Mission church in Uranium City and were among its most staunch supporters. He was asked to teach a Sunday school class, and has maintained a consistent Christian testimony in the ten years or more since he became a Christian.

The aircraft has not only been used to bring salvation to some who otherwise would have no opportunity to be saved, God has used it to save lives physically so individuals would have another chance to accept Him. Once as Marshall and Indian evangelist Tommy Francis were flying out of Dore Lake they planned to stop at a certain mink ranch on nearby Smoothstone.

"Is this Caribou's place?" Tommy asked as they banked to land.

The pilot shook his head.

"No, I just decided to go in here and see these folks instead."

As the plane taxied to shore nobody came out of the cabin to meet them.

"That's strange," the missionary muttered. "I don't think they're away. Too much stuff has been left out." Once ashore they went hurriedly to the house. "Hello!" he called, knocking at the same time.

There was no answer.

"Hello!"

A faint groan came from a bedroom.

"Tommy, did you hear that?"

They went inside. There on the bed lay a woman, her face

a pasty, ashen blue. Even her hands had a blueish cast. She opened her eyes as they entered the little room and her lips parted, but she did not speak at once. She was breathing with great difficulty.

"What's the matter?" Marshall knelt beside the bed and felt for her fluttering pulse.

"My heart," she managed. "I—I didn't think I could make it to the house."

"Has she ever had any trouble like this before?" Tommy asked quietly.

Marshall nodded. It was general knowledge that her heart was bad, but he had never known her to have an attack as severe as this appeared to be.

At that moment her husband came into the house.

"I was out on the lake when I saw you land, Marshall," he started to explain. "I came over as soon as——" The words stuck in his throat. "Her heart?"

"She was lying here when we came in."

"She hasn't been feeling well the last few days," he said. "We were going to take her in to Big River to the doctor in the truck, but our road (40 miles of trail largely through muskeg to the province-maintained gravel) is so bad it'll take us 12 or 14 hours. I've been afraid to risk it. If we'd get stuck———"

They loaded her into the aircraft and in a matter of minutes had her down to Big River to the hospital.

"Marshall," she said weakly as the plane moved across the lake. "God sent you to our place this afternoon."

She was in oxygen all that night and well into the following day. At this writing she is back on Smoothstone with her family, very probably owing her life to the fact that the plane stopped in. Whether the family will make a decision for Christ no one knows, but there is a warmth and friendliness there that had never been so apparent before.

Word of such things have a way of spreading. Not long afterwards, the plane sat down at Beauval and an Indian man sent an urgent message to the pilot to come and see him.

"We've been wondering what to do about this thing," he began, relating the story of two mineral finds he and a friend had discovered when they were trapping years before. "We haven't said anything to anyone about it since we found those places twenty-five years ago. We were afraid they would be stolen from us. But we got to talking the other day and I said, 'that preacher at Dore Lake is one fellow we can trust.' "

And so he related his problem.

Although he thought it was the individual in whom he was putting his confidence it actually was not. It was Christ as He was lived in the missionary's life. It was Christ as He was revealed in the acts of mercy and kindness the missionary performed. And it was the aircraft that put the man of God in touch with so many of the people in the area he served.

*   *   *

Ed Hickey had a pilot's license and his own plane when he and his wife, Marion joined the Mission. After he had been with the NCEM for some time they turned the aircraft over to the Mission. They worked first at Buffalo Narrows where they manned the station. But it was soon apparent that Ed was needed as a pilot. Love for working directly with the people dies hard, however, and the Hickeys tried for a time to maintain their station while Ed flew. It soon developed that there was so much flying for Ed that maintaining the station was impractical. Others were sent to Buffalo Narrows and the Hickeys were transferred to The Pas where Ed devotes his time to flying supplies in to the various stations, hauling missionaries in and out and moving Indian evangelists from one village to another. Ed helps with visitation whenever possible, but his flying load has increased steadily until there is little time for such activities.

With the increased need for flying, Van and Pat Neudorf, who were stationed at Dore Lake, Saskatchewan and conducting a visitation ministry in the isolated area north of that settlement, were transferred to the James Bay area in Quebec.

The Indian families there still travel in groups of three or four families when they go out in the bush to hunt or trap. Van and Pat and their adopted son, Ronnie (a Cree Treaty Indian) visit those camps. Their stay is as casual and unstructured as that of the people they visit. If the response is cold and unfriendly they may visit a couple of hours or overnight. If the people are friendly and open the visit may stretch to three or four days. They have Bible studies and a time of singing if possible.

In the summer when the people are in their villages Pat and Van do a certain amount of visiting but they also help with camps and Daily Vacation Bible Schools. In addition, Van hauls missionaries and supplies to and from the stations along the James Bay coast, relieving Ed Hickey of his responsibilities in that area.

Chapter 12

"Don't tell Barney about this."

Barney stood at the door of the Calverley home in Dore Lake, a strange earnestness on his dark face.

"Are you going down to Big River tomorrow, Marshall?" he asked.

"I'll be going down for the mail as I always do."

"I'd like to ride with you."

Often the missionary was hesitant about taking passengers to town because so many times they were interested in making the trip only to buy liquor. However, Barney seemed to have something else on his mind.

At 8:30 the next morning the two men drove off in the icy winter darkness. They would be almost to Big River 80 miles away before the sun came up. Barney was quiet, almost morose. The missionary noticed it, but was careful about what he said.

"You've got something important to go to Big River about, eh?" Marshall began after a time.

Barney nodded. "There's a fellow there who makes some stuff to boil your traps in," he said. "I'm going down for some."

The missionary eyed him curiously. He had not even known there was a medicine man in Big River, although it did not surprise him. He had lived long enough among the Indians to know that all too often their pagan ways lurked just below the surface of their apparent civilization.

"Somebody has been conjuring against me," he continued

uneasily. "I go to my traps. There are no tracks in the snow and
no new snow to cover them, but the traps are sprung with little
pieces of sticks or wood. No beaver. No mink. Not even any 'rats.
All winter it has been so."

Marshall waited. Barney was taking him into his confidence
in a way that an Indian seldom did with anyone, and especially a
white man.

"I go hunting just like I always do," he said. "I am careful
to get down wind. I move close under cover. But when I get there,
no moose. Just tracks that show he turned and run away. The same
with rabbit—partridge—" His voice caught. "Never before am I
without meat . . . Somebody put a hex on me."

The missionary knew that what Barney said about not being
without meat before that winter was true. He had the reputation
of being one of the best hunters and trappers in the area.

"I have my Bible," he continued in all seriousness. "And at
night I take it to bed with me." The quavering in his voice increased.

"The evil spirits can't hurt me when I have the Book so close."

The missionary at the wheel said nothing for the moment. There would be time later to talk to his passenger about the Word of God. Right then the frightened trapper wanted to share his harrowing experience with one he knew to be an understanding friend.

Then he told what had happened the afternoon before. Another trapper friend had come to visit him and they were still sitting in his clean little shack.

"What's that, Barney?" His friend reached over on the table and picked up a small piece of dried moose meat.

"I do not have any dried moose meat in my house since summer, Marshall," he went on. "Nobody has any dried meat this time of year." His voice dropped hoarsely. "The spirits used that piece of dried moose meat to tell me that that is all the meat I am going to get this winter!"

They travelled another mile or two before he spoke again.

"So I go down to get the stuff to boil my traps in," he concluded. "I will get rid of the hex."

"You know, Barney," the missionary began, his voice gentle and understanding, "there is One who is more powerful than all the evil spirits of Satan—One who cast devils out of men . . ."

Instantly the trapper was interested. Marshall talked to him the rest of the way to Big River. He quoted Bible verses to show his Indian friend that Jesus is the Son of the Living God and is all powerful; that He came to save those who confess their sin and put their trust in Him.

Barney, who had professed to have made a decision for Christ some months before, listened intently.

The missionary didn't ask him to forego seeing the medicine man. That decision would have to come from the trapper himself. But as they drove along in silence he prayed that God would speak to his disturbed passenger's heart.

The medicine man lived a number of miles in the country, but there were taxis available in Big River if he couldn't find a friend to take him out there. Marshall stopped at the cafe for the burly Indian to get out.

"It's now about 10:30," he said. "I'll be leaving to go back to Dore about 1:00. I'll pick you up here."

But Barney did not get out of the truck seat.

"I have changed my mind," he said. "If you will come and pray with me I'll not go to the medicine man. I'll try it your way."

"I'll be over Sunday afternoon," the missionary promised him.

He and his son Ron went to Barney's shack the next Sunday.

Marshall read the Bible to him, explained the verses carefully, and they knelt and prayed with him.

It was six weeks later before Marshall saw him again. There was a big smile on his round face.

"I go back to my trap line," he said, beaming. "My traps are filled with beaver. And when I need meat I shoot moose. . . . I tell my friends in Green Lake that God has done a wonderful thing for me!"

The missionary was hopeful, but still not entirely sure that Barney really knew Christ as his Saviour. Not until Albert and Ada Arcand came to Dore to do personal work did he find out for certain.

"We have talked to Barney many times in Cree," Ada said firmly. "There is no doubt in our minds but that he is a Christian."

The next fall Barney sent his children, Hazel and Freddie, to the NCEM boarding school at the Montreal Lake Children's Home. Later that year the doctor informed him that he had a very bad heart. He waited until Marshall came to see him.

"I want the papers made out so the law will let you take care of my children when I die," he said. "I want them raised as Christians."

For several years Barney continued to hunt and trap but the Lord was beginning to lead him in another direction. He began to talk to his people about their need of the Lord Jesus Christ. When Calverley and his family moved to Winnipeg to take over the Union Gospel Mission there Vander and Pat Neudorf were transferred to Dore Lake. Vander, and Ray Kennedy, who was also stationed at Dore, took Barney with them on visitation.

"I start to talk to the people about their need of Jesus Christ," Barney said, "and if I have a man's ear I keep talking to him. If I don't, I change the subject. There's no use talking to anyone unless he hears what you say."

In order to be better equipped for witnessing Barney went to the Indian Bible school at Lac La Biche, Alberta.

But the lure of the bush was strong for Barney and he kept going back to his cabin on Mirasty Lake until God showed him, unmistakably, that he should be living in Meadow Lake where he could be more effective in serving Him.

Barney's heart continued to give him trouble until he had a slight heart attack while guiding hunters. A little while later he slipped on the ice, fractured his skull and had a severe brain concussion. That ended his living in the bush.

"You've got to be in town, Barney," the doctor told him.

"You're over seventy now and your health is such that you can't live out there alone."

It was hard for him to move to town. Even in so small a place as Meadow Lake cars going by his house bothered him. And he missed the quiet beauty of his home in the bush. But God had work for him to do. He began to visit in the hospitals and on the Reserves near Meadow Lake. He led one Indian woman (aged 84) to Christ and a man of 80 to the Lord.

His reputation as a hunter and a man were of great help to him. One Christian hunter was telling of hiring an Indian guide during the moose season. The guide had taken along his own rifle, although that is against the law. When he heard that his hunter knew Barney Lacendre he was most disturbed.

"Don't you tell Barney about this," he said several times. "Don't you tell him I had my gun along."

It is not easy for Barney to get around, but wherever he goes he has a word for his Christ. Barney loves to "dish it out in Cree."

*　　*　　*

All too often the wonderful truths of the Word of God are couched in stilted terms that have been used so much they have lost a great deal of their meaning. It is indeed a thrill to hear from the lips of one who has accepted Christ from great spiritual darkness the simple statement of his new belief in God. There are few cliches in the words of such a person, and no heavy and all but meaningless phrases. The heart speaks in colorful, if somewhat unorthodox, language.

"I am Joe's wife. Before I got saved he left home quite often. He went to different churches studying and learning about the Bible. Finally one day he bring a Bible home with him. After that when we would go to bed he would lay there reading the Bible. Out loud he would read a verse of Scripture.

"I did not understand nor care to hear anything about the Bible. I wasn't saved yet and my church told me to turn away from it. So I would turn away from my husband when he read. The missionaries came to our house, but I turned away from them, too.

"Some nights I would go to bed and take the Bible to read a Scripture or two. My husband would come up after and catch me. Then he would explain things.

"Finally I see this change in my husband's life. He was not drinking, dancing, gambling and doing all these things people so like to do. I wanted to change, too.

"So I accepted the missionaries in my home as they teach us the Word of God. Finally I knew in my heart that I was a sinner and needed Christ as my Saviour. I needed my life changed as my husband's life was changed.

"Before I was saved I used to get up in the morning and swear something awful at my children. Or I would get angry at my husband and swear at him. I was just miserable most of the time.

"But when I got saved and asked Christ into my heart He changed my life. He lived my life, as he did my husband's life. Immediately He delivered me of swearing at my childrens. It has been years since I have sweared at my childrens. Sometimes I get angry, but it goes away. I ask the Lord to forgive me, and He always does.

"Where we live in the community here, it is hard to be a Christian. My own people—my parents say, 'Why you leave your church? That is not the way we brought you up?'

"I say, 'I don't see youse go to church on Sundays. You couldn't believe in your religion. Weekends the boys go away, having a good time. Sundays they stay in bed. Is that a good Christian life? But if you want to stay away from me on account of me turning my life over to Christ, to go to a church where they preach the gospel of Jesus Christ that is all right. I will *not* deny my Christ.'

"If I am not welcome in my own parents' home, and they do not want me around that is all right. My *Saviour* will not disown me. No matter where I go or place where I work, I will be a witness for Jesus Christ.

"I do not know how I could live before I had Christ as my Saviour. But I know I am a very happy woman today and we have a very happy home. We read our Bibles every day and we look to God for strength and courage. He is the only One who matters in our lives."

*   *   *

The Indian children at Montreal Lake Children's Home have the same sort of problems other youngsters do. On one occasion when Mrs. Deone Gruchy, then Deone Geiger, was matron, one of the little girls was crying in the next room. She slipped into a robe and went in to learn the trouble.

"I'm afraid there's going to be a war," she sobbed.

"Why don't you come in my room and sleep with me the rest of the night?" Miss Geiger said.

The little one stopped her crying momentarily, and nodded.

In the big bed in the room next door the matron opened the Bible and read to her from Psalm 46. " 'God is our refuge and strength, a very present help in trouble.' " She paused momentarily. "Do you know what that means?" she asked.

The little girl said she did.

"Sometimes when I am afraid at night," she said, "I pray for God to send down many angels to make a little house around my bed. The angels all stand around to make the walls and God stands at the top to make the ceiling. Then I go to sleep because I am not afraid."

The same little girl confided that she was concerned about a friend of hers at school.

"I tried and tried to be brave enough to witness to her," she said. "One day I tried real hard, but before I could do it the bell rang and school was called, so I couldn't. When I get to school in the morning I'm going to talk to her, if I get the chance."

That afternoon the same little girl came running into the dormitory from the school grounds.

"Miss Geiger!" she said excitedly. "I did it! I did it!"

She had gone up to her friend and said, "If there was a war here, what would you do?"

"I'd stay here, I guess," the other girl answered carelessly.

"What if you dies?"

"I guess I'd just die, that's all."

"I wouldn't be afraid to die," Esther explained. "I would just go on to Jesus and wouldn't have to suffer. But I do feel sorry for the ones who would have to suffer." She paused for an instant before plunging ahead. "If you died, would *you* be ready to meet Jesus?" she asked pointedly.

"No," her friend admitted, serious for the first time since the conversation started.

The same girl attended high school at Caronport, Saskatchewan in the southern part of the province. She had been praying for her nephew who had been ill. She got a letter from her parents.

In the midst of reading the letter she stopped suddenly and broke into song. "God answers prayer," she sang joyfully.

"What's that all about?" a friend asked.

"God answered my prayer for Gordon. My folks wrote that he's well now."

The faith of many of the converts is thrilling indeed. There is a warmth and freshness about them that shouts of sincerity and a deep personal trust in the Saviour.

Chapter 13

Up the James Bay Coast.

The Hudson's Bay Company is the best known company name in all of Northern Canada. Before the arrival of local government in the last century they were charged with the responsibility for law and order across the vast reaches of the West and North. A bit of their former paternalistic attitude towards the Indians and Eskimos still remains.

When Old Factory, a tiny, wind-swept settlement on an island along the southern lip of James Bay was abandoned and the Indians moved, the Hudson's Bay Company was left with some buildings they no longer needed. Rather than move them themselves they sold them to the Northern Canada Evangelical Mission for a fraction of their value because the material would be used to build homes for those who had come north to minister to the people.

"The only restriction is that the buildings be torn down and moved within two years," the mission representative was told. "We want the material to be put to use."

"They cost thirty or forty thousand dollars," the missionary reported excitedly to the mission board at their next regular meeting. "And we can get them all for a thousand dollars."

The purchase was made and a forty foot launch located and bought to use for moving the lumber. There were two trips made to James Bay by missionaries from the outside, a year or so apart. The first to locate suitable lots for building in the settlements where they had stations or were planning to open stations. The second trip was for the purpose of tearing down the buildings and transporting the material to the places where it was to be used.

John Penner, Tommy Francis, Ronello Knightly and Don Affleck made one or the other. Marshall Calverley and his son, Ron, accompanied them on both trips.

To Calverley it was like a visit home. He had helped survey the area for the mission when they were thinking of opening new stations there. He had been manager at the Eastmain store during his Hudson Bay days. It was there that he first began to learn Cree and came to understand and love the Indians.

"Here in Eastmain," he told the missionaries the first night they spent at the settlement, "I never used to lock anything up. The cash box stood on the counter even when I wasn't in the store. And I didn't have a thing stolen all the time I was here."

He told of being called out of the store when two Indian children were inside and coming back to find them playing with the cash box on the floor. They had money piled everywhere.

"Early the next morning," he went on, "their father came over to see me. He was quite concerned. 'I wanted to tell you that when my boys were playing with the money they didn't steal any of it,' he said.

" 'I didn't give that a thought,' " I told him. " 'I haven't even counted it.' "

He could have told the Indian man that months before he had purposely put a nickle on the counter to see whether anyone would pick it up. It was still lying there, although every person in the village had been in the store and gathered around the counter dozens of times.

There was no drinking to speak of among the Indians in those days, he told his listeners. And it wasn't uncommon for a young man to come into the store after the death of his father and ask how much he had owed The Hudson's Bay Company.

"It was company policy then (and may still be for all I know)," he said, "to advance food supplies to reliable trappers during the off season to be paid for from their next winter's catch of furs. If a man would die owing money to the store no attempt was made to collect his debt.

"Yet I have had young fellows 18 or 20 years old come in and tell me that they would start paying on their father's bill as soon as they could. They would start whittling on it and keep paying until the debt was entirely paid."

One of the veteran missionaries in the group took a deep breath. "I'm afraid the white man has brought more than liquor to degrade

It was there that he first began to learn Cree.

them," he said. Then the look on his face changed. "Now if we can get them to see Christ as the answer to their problems————"

Before turning in that night they prayed for the people who were scattered along the bleak east coast of James Bay.

*   *   *

The work of dismantling the buildngs was begun and the boat crew started hauling the lumber north. They had known it would not be easy. Even the most inexperienced of them knew James Bay by reputation.

The slender inland sea was a restless, temperamental body of water, a lady of many moods when she escaped her winter prison. As though furious at being locked so long in ice, she whips into mountainous waves as the sudden, violent storms of June lash savagely across her. Her temper is only slightly better in July and August before exploding into a rage in September and October that forces even the hardiest of skippers to seek shelter. And before the month is out their sturdy craft are put up on blocks beyond her reach.

She is plagued by reefs that reach for unwary boats with jagged, rocky fingers. The tides are troublesome even to the most experienced James Bay navigator. They alternately expose as much as three miles of shallow mud flats or surge up the many rivers with such force that they temporarily reverse the current. They tug and pull at the boats foolhardy enough to try to use her. If the craft is out of sight of land they can deflect the inexperienced helmsman until he is far off course.

Manning a boat on James Bay was no place for the uninitiated, especially a boat heavily loaded with lumber.

Although the mission crew had an Indian guide aboard who knew the Bay as well as he knew his own trap line, and Marshall Calverley, who had several years of experience on and around it, they had their share of difficulties.

The big boat drew four feet of water, which made it impossible to bring it close to shore in most places. That meant the lumber had to be loaded onto canoes and taken in. They would go in as close as possible with high tide, anchor, and unload furiously in a desperate race to get through and under way again before the tide went out.

On one occasion shortly after the work started they were following this procedure at Fort George where the mission was building a five room house. They had just finished unloading the last canoe ashore when young Ron Calverley pointed out to sea.

"Look, Dad!" he cried.

The tide was running out.

One of the men sprang for the canoe.

"It's too late now. We're caught."

As the water receded the launch was left on the sand with only a few scattered puddles about her. Grinning Indians came down to shore and looked knowingly at the hapless boat. They, too, had been tricked by the Bay. It was amusing to see it happen to someone else. It was not until the next high tide that the crew was able to leave.

But it was the storms that caused most of the difficulties and delays. On one trip a number of Indian volunteers were aboard. Their canoe was lashed to the top of the cabin and a big mission canoe was being towed behind.

Half way to their destination the wind came up. Gentle swells deepened under the lashing of the gale and minutes later the boat was being buffeted by the waves. All they could do was run for the nearest harbor.

The storm came up so suddenly, so violently, that the twenty-three foot canoe began to fill with water and threatened to swamp.

"We've got to pull her up!" someone shouted against the roaring wind.

"She's got too much water in her for that! We'd have to stop to handle her, and we've got to keep headway ourselves or we'll 'broach'!"

They stared at it with momentary helplessness.

"What'll we do? Cut her loose?"

Cut loose a canoe they needed so desperately?

One of the men leaped aboard the floundering canoe and began to bail. The craft lurched sluggishly with each towering wave, but he continued to throw the water out of it with a small pail. As the craft lightened it rode a little higher in the water. The Indians, who lived along the Bay and had experienced many storms, knew what to do next. As soon as he finished bailing they pulled the canoe close behind the boat. He scrambled out and helped them hoist it out of the water to the safety of the top of the cabin. Only then did he stop and fight for breath. But, no matter. A valuable piece of mission property had been saved.

During the melee one of the men lost his cap overboard. Several weeks later they were storm bound on Walrus Island (so-named because of its shape—not the proximity of those unusual animals) where they found the man's cap washed ashore.

"As I think back on those summers," Ron Calverley said, "it seems to me that we spent most of our time running from storms."

The one he probably remembers best happened the first trip when they were stormbound behind an island for so long they ran out of food. As the wind continued to blow day after day stores ran low and the men had to ration what was left.

"For five days," Ron said, "all we had to eat was soup."

It was in midsummer and one of the men thought it might be possible to find some berries ashore. They were all hungry and tired of their monotonous diet.

"I'm not goin'," twelve year old Ron announced. "I hate picking berries."

"The fellows who pick berries eat berries," his dad said. "Those that don't, do without."

"That's all right with me," he retorted bravely. His tone revealed that he didn't actually expect them to find any.

The men were gone for several hours and when they came back they had berries. Some of them weren't too ripe, but they looked delicious to the hungry men. As the cook for the day went to measure them out he looked questioningly at Marshall. They all had heard what he told his son.

There was a brief silence.

"There'll be none for Ron," he said quietly.

The boy swallowed his disappointment, but did not argue with the decision he knew was just.

"I can tell you one thing," his dad said later, "the berries I ate were gall in my mouth. I had to choke them down. But I couldn't let Ron think he could sluff off his share of the work and still enjoy what the rest of us had earned."

Not long afterward Ron Calverley redeemed himself by saving the boat when the anchor dragged free and the wind threatened to carry her across the Bay.

Later the same summer the mission launch was anchored in the river at Rupert House almost a mile and a half from the sea. The men had been visiting in the settlement and that night they were going to have a service. Arrangements had been made for the use of a large building and Tommy Francis was going to speak. They were on their way to the building that evening when there was a sudden flurry of excitement along the river bank.

"Hurry up!" someone shouted in Cree. "Hurry up! *Hurry up!*"

The missionaries turned quickly towards the river. Indians were running in that direction, but Marshall and his companions couldn't see the water for a huge pile of logs.

He dashed between two piles of lumber and past the poles on the river bank. There in the fast water he saw two heads bobbing.

One was that of a lad of ten years old or so. The other was that of a young man who was struggling to keep the boy's head above water. But the tide was running out, making the current doubly vicious. Not too powerful a swimmer himself the would-be rescuer was having all he could do to keep a grip on the boy until help came.

For a flutter of time the missionary was motionless. Everything was happening so swiftly, and yet so casually that it didn't seem real. And yet it was all too real. Men were running up and down the river bank, shouting and bumping into one another. There were boats and canoes close by, but no oars or paddles. Two men shoved a canoe into the swift-moving water and jumped in, trying to paddle with their hands. Somebody else grabbed a pole and held it out, but it was far too short to help.

At that instant Marshall acted. He dove into the water and started to swim towards the two boys. He was only a few feet away from them when the older fellow could hang on no longer. His grasp weakened and the frightened lad slipped away from him.

Marshall saw that and dove, swinging his arms about, frantically.

"The current was so swift," he said later, "and the water was so murky I didn't think I'd find him. I couldn't have on my own. It was the Lord's doing. I closed my hand and his wrist was there!"

He hauled the boy to the surface and swam ashore. Eager hands took the lad and carried him ashore.

The young man who had jumped off the dock when he saw the little fellow in the water found Marshall's New Testament floating nearby and thought it was his wallet. He got it and carried it ashore between his teeth.

The service that night was delayed an hour or so, but when they did hold it about 200 came out.

"We are just opening the station here," Tommy Francis reminded them. "The one who had jumped in the water to try to save him couldn't hold him any longer and had to let him go. There were no boats with oars close by. No one else to rescue him. If the mission boat hadn't been in Rupert House the boy would have drowned . . . ."

He went on to give a spiritual application to the incident that was still so real and fresh to all of them.

"None of us knows how long we have on this earth," he said. "We don't really know how fast death can come. The thing we must do is to be ready, so when it comes we can go to heaven."

The missionaries waited hopefully after the service for some sign that even one individual had been touched enough by what happened and by the heart-searching message to want to make a decision for Christ.

But there was none.

They had heard the words from the lips of one of their own people. They would ponder what he said and perhaps talk about it when two close friends were out on a trap line together, or sitting out a storm behind some island on the Bay.

Missionary work is seldom easy—seldom do the results come with any rapidity at all.

Along the same coast a year or so later Mr. and Mrs. Ted Leschied moved to a station. It was useless for them to try to hold services, and seemingly just as useless to witness personally. But the quiet testimony of Christ in their lives was having its effect.

The Leschieds were the only whites in the settlement to be invited to the 'goose feast,' the biggest event of the year in their village. It marks the beginning of the geese migration, which, like the caribou in other areas, provide the Indians along the east shores of James Bay with most of their meat.

When illness made it necessary for the Leschieds to go out of the North quickly, the Indians gathered around their house to help them get ready and to say goodby.

"We will take care of your things for you," one man assured them.

A woman went up to Mrs. Leschied, tears streaming down her cheeks. "We *want* you to come back!" she said brokenly.

No souls yet, but they have the hearts of the people. All across the North veteran missionaries are becoming increasingly aware—indeed, if they haven't always known it—that first they must win the hearts with love. Then the people will listen to the message of their lips.

Chapter 14

The North is for men,

Mention the North and immediately one thinks of men—resourceful, rugged individuals who can ignore the cold and shrug off hunger and endure back-breaking work. Men who can chop wood like lumberjacks, skin out a moose, or fix the motor on their power-toboggan. But there are also women in the North, especially on the mission stations. Not as rugged physically as the men, perhaps, but as resourceful and stoic about hardships and loneliness.

In a way their part is even more difficult than that of their husbands and male co-workers. They are the ones who have to stay at home, often the only white woman in an entire settlement. They have to keep the fire going, sometimes in a drafty little cabin with wood they may have had to split themselves. They have to bear the ordeal of childbirth alone, forced to go outside for the last months of pregnancy by the isolation of their stations and a lack of medical help in the North. They have to raise their children, often under hostile conditions in the villages, and without the reassurance of doctors, hospitals and an unlimited supply of drugs. When the men on the station are away they have to see that water is drawn, sometimes from a hole in the ice, and carried back to a tiny cabin in temperatures as cold as 60 degrees below zero.

They learn the chill of fear when their husbands don't return at the appointed time, knowing well that they live in a harsh and unrelenting land where death waits for a moment of thoughtlessness, or for one careless mistake.

They have to keep the fire going in a drafty little cabin.

Mrs. Art Tarry had the agony of seeing one of her babies die while the family was at Buffalo Narrows during those hard early years. At first she had been reluctant to go North. She had been very content to remain in a pastorate in southern Canada. But she saw that her husband's heart was in the North and she asked God to make her willing to go there. Once they arrived on the field and she saw the need there was no turning back, not even in the face of tragedy.

" 'Can a woman forget her sucking child, that she should not have compassion on the son of her womb?' " she quoted in an early issue of the mission publication, Northern Lights. " 'Yea, they may forget, yet will I not forget thee.' Isaiah 49:15."

No doubt recalling the ache in her own heart she continued.

"Have you ever seen a mother give her baby away to anyone who would take it, and forget all about it? That is exactly what happens here—without natural affection. This in itself makes getting the Gospel to them so imperative.

"God has not forgotten the poor Indian souls."

"These same little ones, when they reach the age of sixteen, are very often married to some old widower for whom they have no love. As a result, they very often leave their partner and seek for another place to live. This leads to deep immorality, and our land is full of it."

But her compassion, like that of the other missionary wives, did not end with lamenting the situation. Even then, her heart heavy, she was witnessing from door to door.

"Usually we knock before going into a home," she went on, "but if we get no reply we walk in anyway.

"If there is more than one room the mother is seldom in sight. She has been warned often about entertaining the missionaries or their families. I talk to the children a few minutes, and if their mother is in the bedroom I walk in and talk to her there. They are generally quite friendly and pleased that we come to see them until we talk to them about Jesus."

She went on to tell of talking to a certain Indian woman about Christ on one occasion when conviction began to gleam in the woman's eyes.

"I am afraid I go to hell," she admitted.

Mrs. Tarry went on to explain the way of salvation and to show her what was necessary for her to avoid going to hell.

"And I know she understood," she wrote.

Tears rolled silently down the woman's cheeks as she battled with herself. Then, when she seemed to be on the very threshold of accepting Christ as her Saviour her face hardened.

"You go home now," she said bluntly. "Your baby wants to go."

She had counted the cost and had found the price too high to pay.

* * *

Mr. and Mrs. Edwin Heal (nee Anne Koop) were looking forward to the birth of their first child in the winter of 1953. She had come North with him to Stony Rapids after their marriage. They had moved into the little shack he had built to batch in when he first went there to open the station in 1949.

It wasn't the best cabin to start with. Lumber had been non-existent in the isolated little settlement and he had been forced to use packing cases and whatever else was available for the ceiling. It was small wonder it collapsed one day shortly after he came back with his bride.

Heal might have put cupboards in the cabin when he built it had he been able to get lumber easily, but he found it less of a problem to keep his dishes and utensils in boxes than to scrounge for material.

"I would like to have some cupboards, Ed," Anne told him gently.

And so he ordered plywood from Waterways, Alberta to come up on the September barge. The plywood arrived, but before he could get at the cupboards an emergency came up. An elderly Indian woman died and her family asked Heal to build a coffin for her.

"But I don't have any lumber," he protested.

Anne looked at the plywood sheets standing along the wall. It would be at least the middle of June before they could be replaced— if they had the money to order more plywood then.

"Yes, we do, Ed," she broke in. "We have the plywood."

"But that's for your cupboards."

"I can get along without the cupboards."

But neither of them was thinking about plywood or cupboards that bleak winter afternoon. Their joy at the knowledge that there would soon be a little one in their home was giving way to concern.

"You shouldn't be feeling so bad all the time, Anne," her husband told her. "It's not normal."

She smiled weakly.

"I'll be all right." But her voice revealed she was no longer as certain as she had been a few short weeks before. "When the baby's here we'll both forget all about this."

"I'm going to have the nurse look at you again."

The nurse examined the expectant mother as carefully as she could and closed her bag.

"I'm sorry, Mrs. Heal," she said, "but you'll have to go to Prince Albert to the doctor."

"I can't," Anne protested. "I'm needed here."

The nurse's mouth tightened.

"Mrs. Heal, your blood pressure is far too high for the safety of either you or your child. There's a plane coming tomorrow morning. You go out on it." There was a tone of finality in her voice that belayed arguing.

The nurse bundled Mrs. Heal against the minus thirty degree temperature and she was taken on a stretcher by tractor and trailer to the airstrip. The first flight ended at La Ronge where she was transferred to another plane and taken on to Prince Albert. An ambulance met her at the airport.

"In the two months that I was hospitalized," Mrs. Heal wrote from their family journal, "it was impossible for Edwin to come and see me, but we were both living for the day when I would return home with the new baby.

"However, the Lord had other plans," she wrote tersely. "Our little one was buried in Prince Albert. Edwin was unable to be with me. A round trip would have cost no less than a hundred dollars. . . ."

The Heals are now at Buffalo Narrows where they are doing the same sort of work that they did at Stony Rapids.

* * *

When the Collies had first moved to Buffalo Narrows a few rods from Churchill Lake there was never any concern for the safety of the children although they loved to play in the water. It was only ankle deep along the shore and they had no dock. Later, however, they had to build a dock, which gave the children access to deeper water.

Two of their youngsters, Bob and Beth, were playing on the lakeshore with Freddie Peterson (a youngster who lived with the Collies for four years while his mother was in the tuberculosis sanatorium). Bobby was trying to reach a stick in the water when he fell off the dock.

"Gerry!" Beth cried as she and three and a half year old Freddie ran up to the other children, "Bobby fell in the water!"

Gerry ran to get their mother, while Bill, an older brother, dashed to the lake. He got Bobby up on shore, but thought he was dead so he left him there, lying on his back, and ran for help. An Indian lad came along a minute or two later, picked up the limp figure, and began to press the water out of him. It was running from his mouth when Mrs. Collie got there.

She carried him up to the house, her heart faint within her. He must be dead, she told herself numbly. "His hands were limp and his face was so puffed he didn't even look like our little Bobby."

"Here!" a neighbor by the name of Peterson said. "Let me have him."

He laid the boy on the ground and began to give him artificial respiration. Twenty minutes went by and there was no sign of life. Then he gasped weakly.

Geraldine, her young face ashen as she watched, turned to Mrs. Collie.

"Mum," she managed, "God answered our prayers."

That night something else happened in Geraldine's life. She came and told her mother about it the next morning.

"I've decided," she said in hushed tones, "that I'm going to live the rest of my life for Christ. I knelt by my bed last night and dedicated my life to Him."

Mrs. Collie took her in her arms.

"My dear," she answered, "the terrible thing that almost hap-

pened to Bobby, brought real blessing to you. You'll never know
how happy you've made me just now."

*   *   *

It was a deceptively beautiful Sunday afternoon just before freeze-
up. Mrs. Harold Roberts and their three daughters accompanied
Harold across six mile wide Clear Lake to visit a family there.

"Do you think we'd better take coats along?" she asked.

He looked up. There were no clouds in the sky and the lake
was a mirror.

"We won't be gone long," he said.

They hadn't visited long when a cloud bank stole across the
sky and by the time they were ready to leave a light rain was falling
and a faint breeze was rippling the water. They cut their visit short,
affixed a small tarp to the front of the boat to shelter Mrs. Roberts
and the girls, and set out. The rain was increasing steadily.

The wind roared in without warning. One minute there was
an all but breathless hush that scarcely marred the mirrored smooth-
ness of the water. The next the lake was being whipped to a frenzy.
Waves deepened until the crests were blown off by the savage wind
and buffetted the fourteen foot boat until its freightened occupants
were sure it would overturn. Water spilled over the gunwale and was
ankle deep in the bottom of the sluggish craft. Roberts struggled to
keep the bow into the wild waves. The girls and Mrs. Roberts
huddled beneath the canvas, praying silently. Then even that pro-
tection was gone. The wind caught the canvas and whipped it off of
them.

"We were certain," Roberts remembers, "that this was the end.
Except for His Grace it would have been."

Roberts saw two small rocky islands not far away and cautiously
manipulated the boat in their direction. At last they were in the lee
of the larger island and were nearing shore. But the waves were so
high that, as they neared shore, they slammed the boat against a
huge boulder. There was a sickening splintering of wood and water
poured in.

"The boat's sinking!" one of the girls cried in terror.

Although the water poured in the hole they managed to get
ashore. Yet, as far as their safety was concerned, it would have
made no difference. The water was so shallow they could have
walked ashore.

Once on the all but naked little island they were faced with
another problem. It was getting dark, the rain was turning to snow,
and the wind seemed determined to crescendo to new heights.

One of the girls began to cry, but her mother quieted her.

"Let's help Daddy gather wood," she said, shrugging away the chill of the rain and snow that set her body to trembling. "We're going to build a fire to get warm."

Roberts got the tarp, that was still fastened by one corner to the boat, made a shield against the wind, and got the little handful of wet wood together.

"Have you got anything to start the fire with?" his wife asked.

He took a Sunday school paper from his pocket.

"Are you going to use *that*?" the oldest girl asked. They hoarded Sunday school papers carefully.

"We have to," he said. "It's all we have."

There was only one match between them. With a prayer in their hearts he struck the match and ignited the paper. The wood caught and in a moment or two they had a fire. The wet wood burned with a thick, choking acrid smoke that, held by the canvas shelter, swirled and eddied about them.

"Daddy," one of the girls said, "it's so smoky!"

"That's all right," her mother said, putting an arm about her. "When the wind goes down it won't be so bad."

The storm worsened during the long, torturous night. Before morning the ground was white and frozen. The shivering missionary family huddled close to the fire, choking and coughing because of the smoke, but unable to move back because of the driving cold.

Towards morning the youngest child got sick from exposure and the smoke and her mother did what she could to take care of her.

At long last daylight came. Harold Roberts started as he looked at his wife.

"Her face was so puffed and discolored from the cold and smoke," he said, "that I wouldn't have known her." There was a long silence. "Yet she had taken care of the children all night long without thinking of herself, or even once complaining."

*   *   *

At one of the annual missionary conferences in Meadow Lake the Bud Elfords received a radiogram that their home had burned while they were out. Little had been saved from it.

Marge Elford was singularly undisturbed.

"Doesn't it bother you that you lost your home?" one of the women asked her.

"God will provide us another," she replied.

"But you lost all your furniture—all your personal belongings and keepsakes."

Still her serenity did not waver.

"There were some pictures I'd like to have saved," she said. "But the things that are really precious to me are here." She indicated her husband and the children who were playing nearby.

Her simple words voiced the keystone of the lives of most of the missionary wives in the North. They see life and material things in their proper perspective and put the proper value upon them.

The wives of missionaries to the Canadian Indians would enjoy the comforts of a city, the taxis and cars, the doctors as close as the telephone, the supermarkets and good schools for their children without sending them away. They would get as much enjoyment as anyone from a beautiful home with plush furnishings, running water, and central heating and air-conditioning.

Those things they have voluntarily left behind that they might help their husbands bring the gospel of Christ to a people who otherwise might never have the opportunity to hear. Yes, the toughness of the men to hardship is reflected in their wives.

Chapter 15

In places where men ought to be.

The Indians at Shamattawa in northern Manitoba couldn't understand why Helen Hisey, who had just come as a part-time nurse and missionary, wanted a well. Everyone knew that surface water had body and life, while well water was dead. Besides, the river was close by and who knew how much digging it would take to finish the well in the basement of the mission home?

But she had decided the river bank was too steep to climb with two pails of water suspended from a yoke across the shoulders. And, if the project wasn't practical, she reasoned, the former missionary couple who dug the basement and built the house would never have started it. A few more feet and she would have water.

It was comparatively easy to get someone to work for her in the remote Manitoba settlement. Work was scarce and the men were anxious to pick up a few dollars doing anything they could. But her new employee lacked her enthusiasm for the well. He was already familiar with some of the strange projects of the white man like cutting firewood in the summertime and piling it close to the house. Usually he figured that if they were willing to pay for their folly he had no quarrel with them. But this was different.

"Go down in that hole?" he echoed, as though certain his ears were tricking him and she had not asked him to do what he thought she did. "Not me."

She tried to insist, but it was soon apparent that no enticement would be attractive enough to get him to work in the well. So she went down the hole and began to dig while he hauled the dirt out by the bucketsful. Uncounted pails of clay and sand were chopped free and hauled out. Now that the job was started she was anxious to stay with it until it was finished. The hole inched deeper as the hours passed until it was eighteen feet deep and cribbed with poles. Helen paused for a time to rest when she heard a faint trickling sound she hadn't noticed before.

Water! After all that digging. Water! For a moment she waited, expecting to see it ooze up through the dirt at her feet. When it was not forthcoming she set to work again, digging even faster.

It wasn't long until there was a thunderous splitting sound as the cribbing gave way. She had dug under the poles, undermining them and the shale gave way crunching the hole to a fourth its former size and leaving her only space enough to stand. The Indian helper fished her out and made no comment, even when she paid him off. She used water from the river for drinking, abandoning the well.

A registered nurse, Helen Hisey was sent to Shamattawa as a part-time nurse and missionary. She was supposed to be under the supervision of a missionary couple for a time, but they resigned and left the field before she got there. After she spent three bewildering, lonely weeks in the village a Christian Indian girl who had just finished the Bible school course at Island Lake, was brought in by plane to help.

"It wasn't until several years later that I began to see what a difficult time I gave Minnie." Helen remembers.

The white woman knew nothing about getting a house ready for the savage winter that was soon to be upon them. She supposed she had seen houses that had been mudded, but hadn't been observant enough to notice they were any different than her's. When Minnie mentioned that it should be done, she was eager to learn.

"We'll have to have some moss, first," the Indian girl explained. "We'll use that to chink the cracks."

Before they were able to get at the task Helen was berry picking when she found some moss. She came home with a pail full, proud of her accomplishment. But Minnie was unimpressed. "It's the wrong kind."

"Do you know where we can get the right kind?"

"Oh, yes." She spoke quietly, as Indian women do. "I saw some in the bush one day."

Helen already had the moss-gathering expedition planned, down to the washtub to bring the moss home in. Minnie looked at it, but didn't say anything. When the tub was filled with wet, heavy moss it was all they could do to drag it home.

By the time the tubful was used Helen had become quite proficient at chinking cracks. The Indians, however, found the project amusing and called them 'beavers.' Only after the work was done did Helen learn that the people felt they should have hired a man for the job.

When the time came to gather more moss Minnie sighed at the tub her white friend got out. "Maybe we could take a sack?"

They had only been in the village a few weeks when a runner came to the mission house and informed Helen that she was wanted at the Council House by the chief. Minnie went along to interpret.

"You are here as a part-time nurse," they told her. "We don't want a part-time nurse. We want a full-time nurse."

There were other areas of conflict, chiefly because she knew nothing about the Indian people. To be sure she had worked as a nurse at a mission hospital near an Indian Reserve. For $3\frac{1}{2}$ years she had taken care of the occasional Indian patient before answering God's call to the mission field. But now that she was working closely with them she realized that she didn't know them or their ways. She was disturbed by their lack of concern about time and was disturbed about the fact that so few of them took their boots off at the door. She was bothered, too, by the fact that they chewed snuff and so few were interested in hearing about Christ.

"They appreciated medical help," she said, "but they had their own religion and didn't want to change."

At that time she was the only white woman in the community— the nearest living 100 miles down river from Shamattawa.

Helen was soon introduced, somewhat rudely, to the fact that the work of a missionary consisted of more than reading the Bible and singing and preaching to the people. Much of her time had to be spent in the difficult chore of keeping the work done that was necessary in order to live. Water had to be hauled from the river, winter and summer. By spring the task of chopping a hole in the thickened ice was a major one. Cutting wood and hauling it in was a task that soon proved to be too difficult. She hired the cutting done and confined her responsibility to splitting it.

Washing clothes was a difficult task that involved hauling water from the river, heating it in a boiler and operating a gasoline driven washing machine. She soon learned the idiosyncrasies of a Briggs and Stratton engine.

Chimney fires were a spine chilling experience until she learned to clean the stovepipes regularly.

And all the while she was trying to deal with medical problems. Not those of a nurse in a well-staffed hospital, but the emergencies of day to day living. Babies were delivered by candlelight, aching teeth had to be extracted, and there was the occasional emergency. The most tragic was the drowning of a five year old neighbor child who would not respond to resuscitation.

Language study she found time consuming but profitable and translation has provided her most rewarding experiences. On one occasion a hymn was translated into the local dialect and at a following service a woman sang it along with some others. She beamed suddenly.

"Oh, I understand it."

Moments like that make all of the long hours and weeks and months of work seem worthwhile.

Agatha Harder, stationed at Lac La Ronge, Saskatchewan, is another single girl who answered God's call to serve Him among the Indians of the North. She was working in the children's ward of the University Hospital in Saskatoon when she first came in contact with Indian children. Usually, they were so much sicker than the others. Her heart went out to them.

The longer she worked with them the more burdened she became for the Indian people—for the children because they were so often trapped by circumstances not of their making, and for the adults because they needed Christ so desperately. She realized that so often the kids suffered for the sins in their parents' lives. And only the Lord Jesus Christ could cleanse their lives and give them purpose and direction.

Finally, she was accepted as a missionary and spent three terms in the Montreal Lake Children's Home. She learned much about the Indian people she had grown to love, but realized there was much more to learn.

"I longed to talk with the older people of their need of Jesus Christ," she said, "but most of them spoke only Cree, or English so imperfectly they had difficulty in understanding the truths of the Bible in our language."

Still studying Cree culture she spent ten months in intensive study of the Cree language. Learning the language, she discovered, helped break down the barriers between her and the people as nothing else could do.

Agatha, too, spent a period of time at Shamattawa, living with another girl as they worked together to reach the Indians for Christ.

"Although the services were for everyone," she wrote "few

men would come. In the Indian culture the woman stays in the background."

To attend services regularly when women were in charge was so foreign to the men that they could not bring themselves to do it. What she said must not be important, in the eyes of the Indian man, because everyone knew that women were inferior to men. What they said would be all right for the children and the women of the village, but not for the men. So, there was a handicap that the girls faced— a handicap single girls face all across the North. Sending couples would probably have been better, except that there were no couples to send.

Few women outside the North can appreciate the loneliness of the single girls who often are the only white women within miles, and who may go for weeks or months without having the opportunity to see another white woman, let alone talk to one.

Visitation and the distribution of Cree literature make up a portion of the effective ministry of the single girls. As time passes and the girls become better acquainted with the women and children, it is encouraging to see their attitude change. Tolerance changes to friendship and often friendship changes to a willingness to listen to the gospel.

"They are slow to give up their formal religious affiliation," she said, "but they do listen."

And there are those, especially among the teen-aged girls, whom she has had the joy of leading to Christ, and of following up with correspondence.

"Some of the girls I counselled at camp two years ago are in Bible school this year," she said.

Across the North there are other single girls who are preaching Christ to a people who would never hear if it were not for them. Some are in hard places where men ought to be, because of the challenging physical requirements of living in such harsh, forbidding land.

Others work in the office, quietly and efficiently carrying on the detail work of a mission with approximately a hundred missionaries scattered over several thousand miles. Such a one was the late Irene Natress who, handicapped by physical problems, nonetheless gave of herself, unsparingly, in any task that was assigned to her.

Nurse, language and translation worker, general missionary, office worker — single women are fulfilling a vital role as workers together with God among the people of the North.

Chapter 16

"I've learned to appreciate the Home."

"I was sleeping in a tent a few weeks ago," one of the missionaries on the edge of the Northwest Territories wrote in his journal, "when the ground was first starting to freeze. It was cold in the tent as there was no fire. I was tucked away in my eiderdown sleeping bag on top of a wooden bunk I had borrowed.

"I thought I heard a rustling around the tent after I had been in bed for an hour or so, but as there had been quite a few stray dogs around, I thought little of it. I took a quick look around the tent and slipped back into my bag again.

"In the morning I thought I heard the same noise, but I could still see nothing. However, when I got out of bed, there was an Indian boy on the ground beneath the bunk. He must have crawled under the back of the tent soon after I got to bed.

"He had slept on the cold ground without any blankets whatever. He had no coat and very few clothes. Seeing me, he scrambled back under the tent and disappeared without even waiting for something to eat. Most likely he would live at someone's cabin for a day or so at a time, or sleep in the bush, and then move on.

"Pray for the children of the North," he reminded himself at the close of the terse account. "They run around here and there all over. Some of them, I am led to believe hardly know where they do belong. Especially do they need to know of Jesus and His Love."

That is the reason the Montreal Lake Children's Home was founded with Mr. and Mrs. John Penner in charge.

With all the unwanted children in the North, and with the lack of educational facilities it is not surprising that the Lord led in the establishment of the Home. Actually, the home was forced into being. The first missionaries at Molanosa, Saskatchewan were single girls, Anne Koop, Mary Keller and Martha Heppner. They were confronted with the problem of taking care of several boys and girls for a variety of reasons. The mother of one was in a tuberculosis sanatorium and would be there for months. The mother of another died suddenly and there was no one else to take care of her son. A third tired of her husband and, leaving her daughter with him, she ran off with another man. They already had a Children's Home, only they didn't call it that.

When Martha Heppner and a new missionary took over the station they inherited the children living with them at the time. About the same time the Lord was speaking to the heart of one of the board members about starting an institution. As he saw it, it would be expressly for the purpose of caring for such children, and for providing a school for those beyond the reach of the government school system.

While the Board was making arrangements for a piece of ground at Montreal Lake and working out the problems involved in moving the first mission home and a log building, a missionary couple took a teen-aged Indian girl into their home.

The girl was young, but had early been introduced to a life of sin. Her last few years had been sordid and filled with all manner of wickedness. Pitiably, she had little understanding of the reality of sin, or the fact that she was lost and headed for a Christ-less eternity.

But the lives of the missionaries and their consistent Christian witness had their effect. The time came when she saw her own hopeless, helpless condition and accepted Christ as her Saviour and the Lord of her life. The change in her own life was instantaneous and amazing. Today she is working as a nurse's aid in a hospital. Her life is clean, and she has a very real testimony for the Lord.

Her salvation from such a wicked background was an encouragement and inspiration to Mr. Penner and the staff as they launched the Children's Home in July 1952. The same Lord who had worked a miracle in that girl's life could work miracles in the lives of others.

Although funds have never been large God has supplied the needs and no child has ever gone to bed hungry because there was nothing for him to eat. When the first school year started, however, they were far from certain that there wouldn't be a lot of hungry days for both the children and staff.

"We've only got fifty dollars," Mr. Penner told his staff. "And we've got to feed seventeen children for the entire year."

He would sit with his wife in the kitchen of their home and talk over the problems with her.

"It just isn't possible," he said, taking a deep breath. Then he expressed the faith that has kept the Home in operation ever since. "But God led us into this. He will provide our needs."

The time came, and soon, when they had to buy flour. He had been putting it off as long as possible, dreading to dip into their meagre reserves, when a truck pulled in to the grounds.

"You're the boss here, eh?" the driver asked. "I've got a truckload of flour for you. Where do you want it?"

From that day on they had to buy very little flour. In 1964, although they fed more than seventy people, they only bought a single bag of flour.

Other food has come to them in a variety of ways.

On one occasion in a year when their own vegetables were very poor, there was a special prayer request at a Wednesday night prayer meeting.

"We would like to have you children pray for potatoes," one of the staff said. "We're completely out."

The following Saturday a whole truck load of vegetables, including potatoes, was brought to the Home.

The youngsters live in dormitories and staff members have devotions with them, or teach them in Sunday School classes. Many of them have heard nothing whatever of the gospel story. It is all very new and strange to them.

"I was telling a Bible story to a group of boys," one of the workers said, "when one lad broke in.

" 'I want to get right with God,' he said.

"He went on to explain that he had accepted Christ as his Saviour some time before, but had been withholding part of his life. Now he wanted to dedicate his entire life to Him."

There was a girl who came to the Home young in life and had all of her schooling there. She made a decision for Christ and planned on going to high school, but she began to drift from the Lord, got interested in an unsaved fellow, and was married at the age of sixteen.

"We prayed much for both of them," one of the staff said.

Not long after they were married she and her husband went over to the home of the ones who had been burdened for them.

"I've been backslidden," she said, "and I'm out of fellowship with God."

Her husband accepted Christ and she confessed her sin and again determined to walk with Him.

Their home has been entirely different since. She has remained true to her Lord and is trying hard to keep her home neat and clean. Though her husband occasionally has his problems, both they and their children give clear evidence that they are Christian.

Girls who have never learned anything about cooking before are taught to cook while at Montreal Lake. When they are twelve years old they are each given an opportunity to bake a cake. Carefully the cook instructed one 12 year old in each step of the recipe.

"Be sure to separate the whites of the eggs," she was told. "And use only the whites, or your cake won't be good."

Proud, arrogant and independent, the girl went ahead with her cake. She neither asked for advice, nor wanted any. But, unfortunately, it did not turn out.

The cook looked at it.

"Are you sure you followed the recipe?" she asked.

"Yes." Her irritation and dismay were evident.

"And you separated the eggs?"

"Yes, I separated the eggs." Anger caused her voice to rise. "I picked out only the white ones, just like you told me."

One lad was brought to the Montreal Lake Children's Home from his isolated settlement in the bush by plane. Timidly he got out and stared, wide-eyed at the strange vehicle that stood on the wide trail than ran down to the lake.

"What's that?" he asked his companion curiously.

"A car."

His expression became more puzzled than ever. "What's a car?"

Never in all his fourteen years had he been out of the bush. He had never seen a horse, or a cow, or tasted ice cream. And when they took him to town during the Christmas season and he saw the gay lights he could not find words to express his amazement. He talked about it for days.

He could not read nor write and he had never heard the good news that the Lord Jesus Christ came into the world and died to save him. He had come to Montreal Lake to have a home and get an education.

Discipline is unheard of in most Indian homes. When a child is made to mind for the first time in his life he is often rebellious and angry.

"When I get out of here," he says, "I'm *never* coming back."

Yet they do come back. And when they are gone they often

write letters to various friends on the staff expressing gratitude or asking advice.

"I took the Lord as my Saviour when I was at the home," one girl from Churchill wrote. "And I loved Him. But I never realized what it was to be in the Will of the Lord. I have such peace as I had never known before, and I want to serve Him."

But that wasn't her last letter. She went back to her home and was dismayed by what she saw.

"Please pray for my brother. He said he accepted Christ, but he is not walking with the Lord. And also for my sister and her husband. They, too, say they are Christian, but they do not live the way they should."

Another girl who became very discouraged and unhappy while at the Home wrote back.

"I have learned to appreciate the Home after I have left the place. I've come to realize how much the people there have done for me. . . ."

There are disappointments, too. Youngsters who make a stand for Christ only to fall away, and others who remain defiant and unreachable to the very end.

The work, now carried on by the Brethren in Christ, is unexciting and difficult, and the day to day responsibility of feeding, clothing, disciplining and educating a large group of youngsters is all too often unappreciated. Yet the rewards are there in the occasional fellow or girl who makes a stand for Christ, becomes thoroughly grounded in the Word and has a consistent testimony. Then the routine becomes fresh and exciting and wonderful.

Chapter 17

Twenty-three miles to Gift Lake.

Two Cree men stood at the door of the mission house in northern Alberta.

"We want to settle an argument," one of them said to Carroll Hill. "I say you're Indian. Joe, here says you're not. How about it?"

The brawny young missionary shook his head.

"No, I'm white."

Disappointment gleamed in the man's dark eyes.

"But you can't be," he retorted incredulously. "You can cut timber and shoot a rifle and pack moose meat out of the bush and talk Cree the same as we do. Are you sure you aren't just a 'little bit Indian'?"

There was good reason the youthful missionary could handle himself like an Indian. Born and raised in the Maine woods, he had been around lumber jacks ever since he could remember. He learned to fend for himself in the woods in much the same way as an Indian lad does.

His father was a rough, burly man of the woods, intent on hewing his children to his own image. When Carroll was ten years old his dad sent him up a seventy-five foot high pine tree and felled it, as the beginning of his training.

"I'll never forget that day," Carroll said. "Dad would hit the base of the tree with his axe and I'd start down. He'd cuss at me until I went back up. Then he'd start to chop again. I don't know how many times we went through that, but it turned out that I was more afraid of dad than I was of riding the tree down. I'd been whipped by him before. It shook me up plenty and scared me worse than I'd ever been scared before, but it didn't hurt me."

It wasn't long until Carroll and his brothers were climbing trees that were to be cut down and riding them down just for the sport of it.

"Then we got to felling them on the side the climber was on," he said. "You should've seen him scramble to get over on the other side before the tree hit the ground."

Carroll's dad had a purpose in teaching his youngest and smallest son to conquer his fear of high places. There was money to be made by felling trees that stood on crowded city streets. It not only was an exacting task, it required a boy who could work in the tops of the trees. Until he got too big to help, city tree removal became a Hill specialty for him and his father.

"We got big money for that," he said, "but I never saw any of it."

When he was twelve years old his Christian mother took him to special meetings. The message touched his heart and he went forward. A personal worker came over.

"We'll go into the inquiry room," he said, guiding the boy ahead of him. "You wait right here and I'll be back in a little while."

The concerned boy waited, but the personal worker did not come back.

For the next six years he stumbled along, not knowing whether he was a Christian or not, or even whether it made any difference.

His father was one of those individuals who felt that the things his boys learned in the woods were far more important than what they got in school. And education was as nothing when there was money to be earned. Because of that Carroll missed an average of three months' schooling a year and the 8th grade was as far as he got.

By that time he was living exactly as he pleased, despite the concern of his mother. He was addicted to motorcycles and fast cars.

"I'd even taken to finding things before the owner lost them," he said, "if you get what I mean."

Carroll Hill had forgotten God, but God had not forgotten Carroll Hill. When he was eighteen he made the decision he had wanted to make six years before. He got down on his knees and turned his life over to Christ. It was only a few months later that he decided to go to Bible school.

"I didn't have any idea of being a missionary then," he said. "All I wanted to do was to get a little Bible training so I could do a better job of witnessing to the fellows I was working with."

At New Brunswick Bible Institute in Victoria, New Brunswick

two things happened to him that had a profound effect on his life. He met and fell in love with his future wife, Kathy, a beautiful, delicate whisp of a girl who seems as out of place in the North as an orchid on a lumberjack's table. He also became acquainted with the work of the Northern Canada Evangelical Mission.

"God spoke to my heart about the North as the men from the NCEM came to present their work at school," he said. "It wasn't any great earth-shaking event for me, but I knew that it was for me."

Even the training his dad had given him in the woods would be valuable.

The Lord had already been dealing with Kathy.

"I was determined I wasn't going to live the straight-laced life of a missionary," she said frankly, "and I was afraid that was what would happen to me if I went to Bible school. So I rebelled against the wishes of my parents and had gone to work as a stenographer."

Finally she could hold out no longer and enrolled in Bible school. There she discovered what she knew in her heart all along, that God was calling her as a missionary.

Upon graduation they were married, accepted by the NCEM and thought they were to be sent to the James Bay area of Quebec. However, the Mission decided they could better use the young couple at Canwood, Saskatchewan after they had finished language school.

It was there that Carroll discovered that even the exacting demands of his father had not completely prepared him for what he would be facing as a missionary. He was visiting in the area around Canwood one day and came to a home just as the family was sitting down to dinner.

"We'd like to have you stay and eat with us," the Indian woman said. He thought he detected a note of hesitation in her voice. "That is, if you wouldn't mind eating what we do."

"Thank you. I'd like to stay."

They put up a chair for him.

"Hunting hasn't been too good lately," her husband said. "We haven't had any meat for the last several days."

Carroll was properly sympathetic.

"Until I got a skunk this morning," the Indian concluded.

A skunk? Carroll turned slightly green as the woman set the platter on the table before him. A skunk! The odor was unmistakable. Whether that was his imagination or not he would never know, but at that moment it filled his nostrils.

"Help yourself," his host said generously.

The young missionary took a small piece of meat on his plate and gingerly cut it with his knife.

When he got home later in the afternoon his face still reflected the rebellion of his stomach. Kathy stared at him.

"What's the matter with you?" she asked.

"I've just had the longest meal of my life." He grimaced. "I think I'll always be able to taste that skunk."

In time he discovered that skunk meat was not on the regular diet of the people he and Kathy had come to serve.

"One of the hardest things I ever did in my life was to force down that skunk meat," he said. "But when you stop to think of it, those people were being gracious and kindly in asking me to stay and eat. They were willing to share what they had with me."

*   *   *

Even while they were getting established in their ministry in Canwood, Saskatchewan, God was beginning to work in Whitefish, Alberta. For five years Dave Wiens and his wife, a former NCEM missionary had been living in the area and praying for the people. Wiens was a Metis Supervisor for the Canadian Government. He could do little missionary work himself because of the demands of his job on his time, but the needs of the people were heavy on the hearts of himself and his wife. Finally they wrote mission headquarters in Meadow Lake and offered to build a house for a missionary couple if they would open a station there.

John Unger and an Indian evangelist went in for two weeks to survey the situation and see what could be done.

Usually the work in a new field is discouragingly slow. While Whitefish has proved to be no exception in that regard, God honored the prayers of the Wienses and twenty or thirty Indians made professions for Christ during that period.

"When it was proposed that we should move to Whitefish," Carroll recalls, "we really didn't look forward to it. It was hard to leave the work at Canwood."

They pulled their little house trailer to Salt Prairie where they lived until their home could be built.

They hadn't been there long when the spring thaws came. The roads were ankle deep in mud and impassable for either cars or trucks, except those equipped with four-wheel drive. The young missionary waited with growing impatience. He had visited all the homes nearby and was looking to Gift Lake twenty-three miles away.

"I've just got to get over there and see some of the people," he told his wife.

"There's no chance of that until it dries up, so you'd just as well relax."

Several days later the last traces of snow had disappeared, but the leaden skies were still leaking and the roads were worse than ever.

"Kathy," Carroll announced decisively, "I'm going to walk to Gift Lake."

"But it's twenty-three miles," she protested.

He packed some grub and a bedroll and set out in ankle deep mud. The Gift Lake villagers stared at him in silent amazement as he came walking in several hours later. One of their own people might do something like that if there was need enough for it, but a white man! They had never seen that before.

When he completed his visit in the settlement and was about to start back an Indian man came over to him.

"You can ride my horse back."

"That's nice of you, but I might have a hard time getting him back to you right away."

"That's all right. You can keep him and bring him back when you can."

The next trip back with the horse was on Easter Sunday. The ride to Gift Lake and back was worth the effort. There were seventy-eight out to the service.

Not all of the Indians were friendly when they arrived in the area, however. Some of the younger men eyed him and wondered what stuff he was made of. It was inevitable that one of them would undertake to find out. The Hills hadn't been there long when the test came.

A belligerent young Cree a head taller than Carroll swaggered up to the missionary while his admiring friends watched.

"I think I c'n whip you," he leared. His fist was cocked menacingly and his jaw was thrust out.

Hill had seen men like that back home in Maine. Let him have any sign of hesitation that he could mis-read as fear and there would be serious trouble.

"This would be a good time to find out," the missionary retorted calmly. He took off his coat without pausing and laid it on the ground behind him. Powerful shoulders bulged from beneath his wool shirt and he stood with his legs slightly apart in the stance his dad had taught him. "Of course," he added quietly, "my dad was the heavy-weight champion of New Hampshire for a long time."

He could have added that his father had quit boxing only after almost killing a man with his fists in the ring.

Now it was the Indian who hesitated. Carroll did not move nor speak for fear he would do something inadvertently that would make his challenger feel he had to fight or face the ridicule of his companions.

"Well——" The fellow's fists relaxed slightly. "Well, maybe your dad was the heavyweight champion of New Hampshire, but you don't look so tough to me."

He stepped back and the crisis was over.

"You wouldn't have fought with him, would you, Carroll?" Kathy asked when he related the incident to her that evening.

"Of course not," he said. "That's no way to settle anything. And besides, it would ruin our ministry here if I had. But I had to let him see that I'm not afraid of him." He sat down and put his moccasin-clad feet up on a chair. "That was the only way to keep from having more trouble with him."

Word of the confrontation must have spread because it didn't happen again.

*   *   *

Although the Hills hold services regularly in Cree it seems as though the most effective work is in visitation.

One aged Indian man listened in amazement as he heard the gospel in his own tongue.

"I have never heard this before," he said. "I have never heard this before."

Carroll explained the way of salvation to him carefully and left him with a Cree New Testament to read. The next time the missionary visited him he was ready.

"I want to become a Christian," he said.

After praying with him and counselling with him Carroll arose to leave.

"Be sure and read your Bible regularly," he said.

"I have been," the Indian replied. "Since you gave the Book to me I have read it. I read this part, and this one, and I've started on this one."

He had read all of the books of John and Romans and was well into First Corinthians.

"It was no wonder he was under conviction and ready to make a decision for Christ," the missionary observed.

*   *   *

Their first summer at Whitefish, the Hills became concerned about having a Bible camp for the young people of the area. They had helped with camps during their Bible school days and knew that such a program could have a lasting effect on the lives of the campers. Other missionaries in the North, including some NCEM

One aged Indian man listened in amazement.

couples, had had Bible camps with good success. Indian Evangelist Bill Jackson, among others, spent most of each summer helping with camps.

"Do you think we can do it?" Carroll and Kathy asked the Wienses.

"If Bill will come up, it shouldn't be too much of a problem," the Metis Supervisor said. "And of course Mary and I will do all we can."

Enlisting the aid of Jackson, Raymond Sparklingeyes and several others, they found a campsite and began to lay their plans.

They set a fee as high as they thought the traffic would bear— $2.00 each for the week.

There were no buildings on the campsite. Jackson had two fairly large tents that could be used for the girls to sleep in, two for the boys, and a third to serve as a chapel. The cooking was to be done on small fires under the sky.

The land itself was no problem. It belonged to the Crown. Conveniently, a wildcat oil drilling outfit had cleared an area large enough for a ball diamond in order to drill several test holes. There was a lake with a sandy beach nearby for swimming. The road into the area was not too good, but the people were used to that.

They went to all the houses in the area to talk with parents and children about camp. There seemed to be a little interest, but there was no way of knowing how many would show up.

"We may have a camp without any campers," Carroll told his wife a few days before the camp was to start.

"There'll be campers," she said confidently.

"Just how many are we to prepare for?" he asked. "Answer me that."

She hesitated. That was something she had been thinking about. The camp was being held ninety miles from a grocery store over ungravelled roads that were rutted and unmaintained. There was no running to the supermarket if an error in ordering had been made, or if an additional twenty campers arrived at the last minute.

Sixty or seventy young people showed up, about half of them with their two dollars.

"They don't have their money, Carroll," his wife said softly, "what are we going to do?"

"We're not going to turn them away, that's for sure."

In addition to those who stayed in Jackson's tents there were others who came in family groups. Two families spent three days travelling each way in covered wagons, covering over sixty miles of back-country trails and roads.

"One girl was a Christian," Kathy Hill explained. "As far as we know, none of the others are."

A hundred and thirty or so came in families. Fortunately the families had their own food and took care of their own cooking. As it was Mr. and Mrs. Wiens made a sizeable donation and the Hills used part of their support money to make up the deficit.

But the results were encouraging.

A young Metis we will call Clarence discovered that the biggest decision he ever made in his life came about because he went to that camp. He drank and smoked and gambled and lived as loose morally as it is possible to live. He had no pride—no shame.

Camp didn't really appeal to him. He went out of boredom—because there was nothing else to do.

Never very clean, even as a boy, the dirtiness of his life was reflected in his outward appearance as he got older. His clothes were filthy and torn and smelled of stale body. He seldom washed or shaved or cut his hair. Looking at him one would have guessed him to be far older than his twenty-four years.

As the week went on Clarence's interest was kindled. And before the camping period was over he had confessed his sin and put his trust in Christ for forgiveness.

But that was not the end of it. Once he cleaned up on the inside he cleaned up on the outside, as well. Overnight his clothes became clean and he kept them that way. He shaved, washed and got his hair cut regularly. It wasn't easy for him to withstand the pressures of his old friends who ridiculed him, persecuted him, and tried to taunt him into drinking again. But, stand he has. He has been in church every Sunday and wants to go to Bible school.

*   *   *

There were results among the younger people at camp, as well. Two sisters wrote to the Hills after going back to their homes.

"Dear Mr. & Mrs. Hill:

"I teach the little kids Sunday. Ever day I thank the Lord he had give me work to do for Him. Please pray for us and we will pray for you. The Lord bless us all.

From Alvina Ward

"Dear Mr. & Mrs. Hill:

"How is you guys? Well, I am fine with the Lord Jesus Christ in my heart. I thank the Lord he had forgive me my sins. Me and Alvina we read our Bibles every day. I been learn the Cree reading mostly every day. I know little but the Lord help me to know it soon. We sure miss you guys when we come home. I hope we will see you again some day.

Goodby
From
Dora Ward."

Chapter 18

Ammunition is their prime responsibility.

Strangely enough, a number of missionaries to the Canadian Indians actually wanted to go elsewhere first. So it was with *Phil and Margaret Howard. After graduating from Prairie Bible Institute where he felt definitely called to do Bible translation, he turned his attention towards South America. There was no chance whatever of getting into China where he had long dreamed of going. The Communists had very effectively closed that door. Now the door to South America closed as well.

It was only then that they became increasingly aware of the fact that there was a need among the Indians of the North that some might say is greater than that of certain foreign fields. Moreover, there were tribes without a written language and the Word of God.

"We had very little financial support pledged to us when we left our home in New Jersey," Howard said.

They were aligned with no mission at the time and the only help that had been offered them was an unstipulated amount from the Sunday school of their home church.

"I was prepared to go to work to support ourselves if that was necessary."

Actually, he only worked a single week on a part-time job for the Army at Fort Nelson.

"Even then," he said, "I didn't find it necessary to take the

---

* Son of the late Philip Howard Sr., long time editor of the Sunday School Times and brother of Betty Elliott, whose husband was killed by the Auca Indians in Peru.

job because we were desperate for funds. The Lord has taken care of us in a wonderful way from the very beginning." •

A survey trip up the Alaska Highway put Howard in touch with the Phil Wilsons, Alliance missionaries at Fort Nelson. There he found a field and a responsibility.

"There's room enough for you to work among the Slave Indians, too," Wilson said. "And especially in the field of Bible translation. It's desperately needed."

There would have been certain personal advantages to living in Fort Nelson, but the Slave Indians there speak a certain amount of English. For that reason the Howards decided upon a more remote settlement where they would have to use the Slave language entirely in speaking with the people. A three hundred mile survey trip down stream (north) took Howard to Nahanni, a small Slave settlement in the Northwest Territories where the Nahanni River joins the Liard.

A professing atheist trader from Nahanni took all of their belongings down river with the boat on which he was transporting all of his own supplies for the winter. And, strangely enough, he refused payment. A local trapper and prospector who had an Indian‧ wife permitted the Howards to use a small cabin next to his own. It not only provided them with a place to stay, they had his wife, Mary, to begin teaching them Slave.

Phil Howard and his family had been on the field a couple of years when they faced their first medical crisis. Phil took sick that summer of 1955 with an infection they could not identify. There was no two-way radio to call for help and no aircraft to take him out.

"We could only commit it to the Lord," he said.

Although they had no way of knowing it the answer to their prayers was already on the way. A day or two later a boat party from Calgary stopped in. They were on vacation and one of the men was a doctor.

"You have a kidney infection," he diagnosed. "I'm sorry I don't have the particular medicine you need." He named the drug. "It isn't common. In fact, I don't suppose there is any within several hundreds of miles of where we are now."

Howard's forehead wrinkled. The drug sounded familiar.

"What did you say that name is?"

He repeated it.

"A doctor friend of mine gave me a large assortment of drugs before we came down here," he said. "I think that's one of them. We didn't know what it was for so we shoved it back in the medicine chest.

Margaret got the bottle. The doctor took a quick look at it, wrote the dosage on the label and when he and his party left he was shaking his head in amazement.

Of the group in the house that night only the Howards weren't surprised. They thanked God for providing the means of taking care of this particular infection in a very wonderful way, and at the same time bringing glory to His Name.

Phil and Margaret Howard, who had operated independently for several years, were in touch with the Northern Canada Evangelical Mission. They came down to Meadow Lake for several of the annual July missionary conferences and finally came into the NCEM.

"We have felt," Phil wrote, "that it has been a distinct advantage, especially in our language work."

Their translation efforts have been interspersed now and again by trips to the Slave settlements for personal work among the Indians. At first they went by dog team in the winter and by boat in the summer. Now an aircraft flown by a co-worker cuts the time to a fraction of that taken for transportation when they first came to the North.

In seventeen years in the Mackenzie River area of the Northwest Territories the Howards have witnessed several professions of faith, but only one or two among them standing firm in the Christian life after a period of time. Although such results could be discouraging to some, Howard sees the work as a battle against the powers of Satan.

"We're attacking the very fortifications of the evil one," he said. "They've got to be softened and broken down just as the fortifications of an enemy stronghold must be destroyed before an army can move in."

He sees their primary responsibility as providing ammunition for the missionaries who will follow. Ammunition in the form of a written language and the Scriptures translated into Slave. That work is going steadily forward with the close cooperation of the missionaries of various groups in the area.

In translating the Book of John into Slave, Howard had the assistance of a young Indian convert of another mission operating in the Hay River area. Being a Christian he had a vital interest in the work and was most valuable.

The final draft was checked by Willie McLeod, a white man of Fort Liard, one of those unusual individuals who understand the language and the people as well as they do themselves.

Willie's grandfather came to the Northwest Territories from Scotland to work for the Hudson's Bay Company. His father was born in the North and also worked for the Hudson's Bay Company.

Ammunition in the form of Scriptures translated into Slave.

Willie not only was born in Fort Liard, he has never been out to so-called civilization. He got his education at the Anglican school in Hay River. His familiarity with the Indians and their tongue got him a job as a police interpreter which he held for years.

"He reminds one of the interpreters in the United Nations," Howard said. "He can interpret as fast as he can talk without any hesitation and fumbling."

What better background and training could one have for assisting with Bible translation? It is small wonder that Howard felt the Lord had guided him to Willie who checked the Book of John for accuracy and helped with the translation of Luke.

There are two books of the Bible in the Slave language to be used by the new missionaries who, even now, are coming in to work among the Slave people. And the translation work is only getting under way. What greater contribution could a couple make for the cause of Christ? They are glad now to have the help of a Wycliffe Bible Translators' couple.

*   *   *

Like so many phases of the Lord's work, that of language is

seemingly dull and uninteresting. The missionaries who devote their time to language study seldom see the spectacular conversions others tell about, or have experiences that bring the listener to the edge of his chair.

"If someone gets excited because you have just discovered that a certain sound in Chipewyan or Chilcotin is made by placing the tip of the tongue on the roof of the mouth," Murray Richardson said, "you can be sure you are talking to another linguist. Other people couldn't care less."

Yet language study, analysis and translation are the cornerstones upon which any effective work for Christ in a new language must be built.

Two NCEM missionaries were working with Cree informants in a linguistics course some years ago. They thought the Indian women who had been helping them were homesick, and that they were talking, between themselves, about how badly they hated the place. As the missionaries got farther into the language, however, they learned what the women had actually been talking about. They were discussing their waistlines and how fat they were getting eating all the rich food.

In such cases the mistake is only humorous. In the realm of the spiritual, it could be tragic. One Indian who had heard the gospel many, many times in English without response accepted Christ shortly after he began to hear it in his own language.

"Now," he said, eyes lighting with the wonder of his new faith, "I understand."

Murray Richardson, who headed the NCEM language department for several years had been working in Chipewyan for some time and began to translate the Book of Acts into that language.

"How do you say, 'it is more blessed to give than to receive'?" he asked his grizzled old informant in English.

The fellow frowned.

"If you get something you'll be happy," he said in Chipewyan.

Murray asked him again. Again he got the same answer. There was no doubt that the informant understood, but his own worldly philosophy was showing through. Murray phrased the sentence in Chipewyan himself.

"Now how would you say it in good 'Chip'?"

The fellow repeated the sentence, cleaning up the grammar and expressing it in a way that is easier to be understood.

The same informant didn't like it when Paul and Silas had been persecuted and beaten by the mob.

"That is not a good story," he said "Let's make Paul and Silas clean up on that bunch of guys."

Painstakingly Murray explained to him why they couldn't change the account. And so the translation continued, slowly, a phrase or a sentence at a time.

*   *   *

When Phil Howard and his wife, Margaret, began to work with the Slave Indians they realized how difficult it was going to be to develop a solid, lasting work without the Bible in the Slave language. They set to work developing a written language for the people and starting the translation. The Gospel of John is now in the hands of the American Bible Society and is being published.

Although Phil and Margaret still are burdened for the Slave tribe they know so well, God has led him into another avenue of service with the NCEM. From his position on the Board of Directors of the mission he was elected General Director. Since that time he has moved to Hay River, Northwest Territories where he can have better transportation and still remain in contact with the Slave people.

*   *   *

NCEM missionaries are working in the Chilcotin, Dogrib, Chipewyan and Slave languages. None of those languages had been reduced to writing before the NCEM work was started. The Slave language is written now and translation work is progressing. So is Chipewyan. The other two languages are being worked on, but are not as advanced. Since the Cree language was reduced to writing by James Evans, a missionary of the Wesleyan Missionary Society in 1840, the work in Cree today is in translating or writing in that language.

To those who are doing language work, it is unspectacular, and sometimes exasperatingly slow. Yet with each book that is translated the work of the other missionaries is made easier and more effective. And so, despite obstacles, it continues——because it must.

Chapter 19

A bag of tea instead.

Cliff McComb and his wife were walking back to their log cabin after the Sunday service at Round Lake, Ontario.

"I've been trying to make the messages as simple as possible," he said. In spite of himself his discouragement showed through. "But Elijah has so much trouble with English I'm afraid he's not able to understand what I'm saying, let alone interpret it to the others."

Ingeborg listened patiently. She had been a missionary to Africa and had seen how hard and discouraging a new field could be.

"Do you suppose they're getting anything at all?" he persisted. "Do they have the slightest idea what I'm talking about?"

"That is not our responsibility, Cliff," she reminded him. "God is the One who must unlock their understanding and their hearts. And He will. It's what we've been praying for."

The hurt was deep in the lanky missionary's eyes.

"If we could only make them know that we *love* them."

It all began when a friend of Marshall Calverley's Hudson Bay days wrote to him.

"I've just been stationed here, Marshall," Art Lellava wrote. "This place is ripe for the kind of work you're doing."

Another group had been working in the area for some time although without visible results, and their veteran missionary would welcome help.

Mr. Lellava came down to the dock to meet the plane when

133

Marshall flew in with Collie and McComb. He was friendly enough, but disturbed.

"I thought a single man was coming," he said. "There are only two houses available in the entire settlement and neither one of them is suitable for a man with a family."

McComb was undisturbed.

"Ingeborg has lived in mud huts in Africa," he said, "without doors or windows—just holes for light, and a mat hung over the doorway. We'll make out."

"Well, I'll show you the houses, but they sure aren't much."

He hadn't been exaggerating the condition of the cabins that were available. The first was just some poles piled together with a rough board floor. The missionary looked it over.

"I'm afraid it would be easier to build a new cabin than it would be to fix this one up."

"It's not too good, eh?"

"What's the other one?"

"It's a little better," the Hudson Bay manager said, "but it's only one room and it's terribly small."

He led McComb and Marshall Calverley to a tiny log building with an attic and a spruce bark roof.

It was decided that they would move into the smaller cabin until they got a house of their own built. Only one Indian in all the settlement could speak any English, but the others came up to McComb.

" 'Wache,' " they would say. "Greetings."

While he was struggling to learn their language McComb was repeating over and over again in his simple messages, the story of salvation. Through the interpreter he assured them that he and his wife loved them and wanted to help them.

McComb not only had to build the house, he had to build furniture, as well. Yet he always had time for those who came to see him. While he was working the Indians would drift over singly or in groups, to ask questions and to talk. On occasion he would keep on working while he visited with them in his newly learned language. Other times he would sit down in the sawdust with them to talk about the things of God.

Isaac, the one who later brought Albert Tait to McComb, was the first to accept Christ as his Saviour. The missionaries had been in the settlement for several months when he came to work for the Department of Indian Affairs. He could speak English fairly well and used to visit with the McCombs and interpret for them.

He led them to a tiny log building with an attic and a spruce-bark roof.

Late in November he made a decision for Christ. Not long after that Albert Tait came to Round Lake and was saved. The two of them had a great burden for souls and spent their time going from one house to the other talking about the Saviour. Isaac would invite those who were interested to his house for Bible study, and later would bring them to the missionary to have him answer their questions. Soon they were coming to McComb every week, and sometimes several at a time.

"We did not try to keep track of numbers," McComb said. "We were interested in them really coming through for the Lord and going on to walk with Him."

A short time later Marshall flew board members, Collie, Tarry and Nish in to Round Lake to look over the station.

"There was a power generator in the settlement and we thought we would show some colored slides the first night we were there," Collie said. "But people started coming to the building by entire families until they were jammed into every available space."

When everyone was in that could get in the interpreter said, "We've come to have you tell us more about the gospel."

"We never did show the pictures."

When the missionary family first went to Round Lake practically everybody in the settlement smoked. The store would be blue with smoke and often the McComb's Indian visitors would smoke in their home.

"We didn't forbid it," he said. "Our concern was to have them see that they should make a decision for Christ. There would be time enough for growth after that had taken place."

One night in midwinter Isaac came over to the missionary's home.

"How does it look for a Christian to smoke?" he asked of Ingeborg McComb when he learned her husband was not there.

"Why don't you wait and ask Cliff about that?" she suggested. "He'll be here in a little while."

In a short time the missionary came in and explained that while the Bible does not mention smoking it is a dirty habit.

"The Bible says we should come out from among them and be separate," he exclaimed, "and tells us that we shouldn't touch the things that are unclean."

Isaac listened intently as the missionary gave him Scriptures on which to base his need for separation.

"If that's the case," he said at last. "I'm not going to smoke any more."

Word of Isaac's decision to quit smoking spread and others

in the settlement began to quit. It wasn't long until there were so few in the village who still smoked that The Hudson's Bay Company wasn't able to sell any tobacco. And the day came when they sent out on the regular plane several cases of tobacco that did not sell any more at Round Lake and took it to another settlement where it would move.

When the Indian agent came in to Round Lake to 'pay treaty,' a big event in the villages of the North, he offered the chief the traditional pound of tobacco.

"I don't smoke any more," the chief said, "so why don't you give me a bag of tea?"

"I never heard of anything so ridiculous," he snorted.

"Our lives are different now that we've taken Christ as our Saviour," they told him.

The Indian agent flushed.

"Well, I'll see you all at the dance tonight."

"There isn't going to be any dance," the chief said.

"There's *always* a dance the night we pay treaty."

"We don't allow dancing in the village any more."

The Indian agent glanced in the direction of Missionary McComb's house.

"I suppose *he's* the one who got you to do a thing like that."

"No," the chief said. "He had nothing to do with it. The Lord is the One who made the change here at Round Lake."

"In the spring of 1953 many had been saved," McComb recalls. "As souls came through for the Lord they were burdened for their friends. I had never seen anything like it before. I would walk through the village and see people reading their Bibles and studying wherever I looked. Some were alone, sitting in the doorways to their homes, or under the trees. Others were in groups. There was a real hunger for the Word."

There was such a hunger that it was decided to put up a building for Bible school and church, and also another house. Men were chosen as deacons and much work was accomplished.

It was during this time that a group were studying the Bible in Isaac's house. Time seemed to exist no more and the discussion went on until long after midnight.

"One man got so under conviction," McComb said, "that his pipe shook in his mouth."

Later he made a decision for the Lord and walked in a way that brought honor and glory to God. Not long after that he and his son were drowned near the village on a very windy day. That had a profound effect on the Christians in the settlement.

The revival continued in the Round Lake area as God touched one heart after another. At Christmas time, 1954 Alex Kenequanash came in from his trap line with a request.

"I want to bring my family in from trapping," he said. "I want to attend Bible school. Could the plane come and get them?"

"We can radio and see, but they're very busy."

No plane was available so he set out again on his snowshoes. It was forty miles out to the cabin where he was living with his family.

"One night when the temperature was well below zero," McComb wrote, "we were leaving our house to go over to the Bible school when we heard a baby crying out on the lake. I told some of the Indian men and they went out to investigate. It was Alex and his family."

The Indian man and his wife had brought their three children and came in from the trap line. Alex pulled a small toboggan with their supplies and two of the children. His wife carried the baby. They had walked the entire distance, spending one night in the bush with no shelter. They built a fire for warmth and gathered a few spruce boughs to rest on. They had come in so Alex could take the Bible classes.

That same winter when school was half over Alex came to the missionary again.

"The Lord has been talking to me about going over to a village where some of my relatives live," he said. "I feel that I ought to go and tell them that Christ died for their sins, too."

The missionary hesitated. Alex was just getting into the Word in Bible school. Humanly speaking there was much to warrant discouraging him from leaving.

"If God is laying this on your heart, Alex, I can't urge you to stay here," McComb said. "I think you ought to obey the Lord."

Alex left Round Lake on the 90 mile trip to the other village. It was a long, wearying journey through the snow. There were no roads. Only an Indian trail from lake to river and across the frozen muskeg to another lake.

When the new Christian got there his people were glad to see him, but were not friendly to the gospel. He stayed for a few days, talking to them when he had the opportunity. At last they became interested in the things of Christ and he was able to lead several of them to Christ.

"You come back to see us in the spring," they told him when he was ready to leave. "We want you to teach us more of the things of the Lord."

They sent a gift of money for the missionary, some money for Bibles and hymn books, and some moose hide as a little thank offering to the McCombs for bringing the Gospel to the people.

"Later that spring," the missionary said, "we used the money they had given us to send Alex and his family back among them so he could tell them more of Christ."

Shortly after the spring break-up in late May of 1955 Alex and his family came back to Round Lake by canoe. But they were not alone. All of the folks from the little village were along—several canoe loads. They all had come to know the Lord Jesus Christ as their Saviour, except for one little boy who was far too young to understand.

"We have come to spend the summer at Round Lake," they explained. "We want to study the Bible with you."

Alex later went to the Bible school at Island Lake.

The McCombs have since been moved from Round Lake, but have visited the people on several occasions and rejoice that many are walking with the Lord.

"It is a real encouragement to see these dear folk still pressing on with the Lord after many years," he said. "Some have gone on to their reward. Others have come to know the Lord. It is proof that God's Word shall not return void."

Chapter 20

I didn't give it to him strong enough.

Albert Tait went to Bible school at La Ronge, as well as at
Island Lake. He only had a grade three education, and the classes
were in English, but he finished at the head of his class. When he
graduated from the La Ronge Indian Bible School he was moved
back to Island Lake with his family where he helped with the Island
Lake Bible School and pastored the local church.

The people in the settlement did not take quickly to strangers.
Albert was one of their own. Yet they viewed him, also, with ill-
concealed suspicion and distrust. He was quite different from the
others.

He did not drink or smoke, for one thing. He spoke neither
of the old ways which their fathers taught them, nor the ways of
good works which they had grown accustomed to hearing.

It was not easy for them to understand this business of pleasing
God which he talked about.

The talk of sin could disturb a man and keep him from sleeping.

The Bible school students spoke of such things, as well, but they
came and went. Albert made his home at Island Lake. For many,
having him there was far from comforting.

Most of the parents allowed their children to go to Young
People's, Sunday school and church, thinking that would be the
end of it. When their sons and daughters came home to tell that
they had accepted Christ as their Saviour and were going to walk
the way of the Christian, some of the parents were furious.

They paddled their slender canoe across the stretch of rough, white-faced water.

"You're not to go back there!" fathers raged. "You're not to go to that church any more!"

One concerned lad came up to Albert after a youth meeting where the Indian evangelist had stressed the burden of sin. "I don't know whether I can be a Christian or not. I'd like to, but my father said he would beat me if I did."

Silence gripped them.

"Who should we follow?" Albert asked him. "Our fathers or Jesus Christ?"

With that Albert waited in silence, letting the boy think about what he had said.

At last the lad knelt and began to pray, asking God to forgive him and save him.

* * *

Albert would take Rhoda, his wife, or one of the Christian men with him to visit the homes in the settlement as often as his teaching responsibilities permitted. Gradually the people got acquainted with them and began to call on them when there was a need.

One evening Albert and Alex Kenequanash, who by this time lived next door, had just finished supper when an elderly man from an island several miles away came to them.

"Our granddaughter is sick," the gray haired man said excitedly. "Won't you come and pray for her."

Albert got up. "Come with me, Alex."

They left immediately, paddling their slender canoe across the stretch of rough, angry water between the islands. When they reached the old couple's cabin they found that the little girl, a year or so old, was lying listlessly on her tikinakun (cradleboard). Her thin face was pale, save for the fever-flush in her cheeks.

The child's grandmother hovered nearby, gnarled brown fingers nervously working the blanket or the caribou-hide ties on the tikinakun. The child whimpered restlessly. Albert knelt beside her and clumsily touched her on the cheek.

"Since before yesterday she has been like this," the old woman said in hushed tones.

Albert had seen his own children lie in much the same way. He hadn't seen any of his family quite so sick, but sick enough so he knew the helplessness that swept over the grandparents.

"Will you pray for her?"

"We'll pray, but before we do, we want to talk with you about Jesus."

The old couple listened quietly as he started at the beginning and explained about sin. He told them how a man must confess the sinfulness of his own life and put his trust in Jesus in order to become a Christian.

"If you will believe, you will see how God will bless."

Questioningly the man and his wife looked at one another. It was apparent that this was completely new and foreign to them, something they had never before considered.

"We don't want to decide tonight," the grandfather said at last. "Maybe we will tomorrow. If she gets well, we might decide to follow Jesus, ourselves."

Albert and Alex knelt and both of them prayed for the sick child.

"We'll be over in the morning," Alex told them as they went out the door.

"And we'll keep praying for her."

The next morning when the two Indian men went back to the home where they had prayed for the child they discovered that she was bright-eyed and alert. The flush of fever was gone from her cheeks. The cradleboard was propped along the wall, the baby strapped in it, within easy reach of the grandmother's loving hand.

"She's better," Albert said, hunkering down in front of the child.

As though in answer, the little one smiled.

"She's a lot better," the old man replied.

"About twelve o'clock last night she started to act different," the old woman added. "I think she was well then."

Albert and Alex sat quietly on the floor of the little cabin, leaning against the outside wall.

The house was clean, but almost bare of furniture. A wood heater, rusted and leaking smoke, stood against the opposite wall. There was only one chair. An old fish box turned on one end served as the other. The table was a piece of plywood with small birch logs for legs. The bed was a pile of blankets and an old mattress in one corner. There was the inevitable grub box near the table.

Albert saw that there was very little food in it. It was much like his grub box at home, he thought idly.

"I don't have any money to pay you anything," the grandfather said uneasily. "Would it be all right to give you some pemmican?"

"You don't have to pay us. We were glad to come."

The old man's expression changed. "You don't want any money for what you did?"

"We couldn't take money for praying for your granddaughter," Alex Kenequanash put in.

Albert picked up his Bible bag. "Now, are you ready to become a Christian?"

The baby's grandfather squirmed. "Maybe some other day."

When the two men were outside Albert glanced at his companion.

"They fooled us that time. I was sure they would want to follow Jesus."

"Yes," Alex replied. "They fooled me and they fooled you, but they won't fool God. One day He's going to say to them, 'Come. You aren't going to live any longer.' Then they'll find out who they have fooled."

* * *

As the months went on and Albert got to know the people better they began to look forward to his visits. This was especially true of some who were attending services. It meant that he had to do his visiting in the evenings after spending the day teaching at Bible school.

Emile and Rose were two who liked to have him come and visit. They had been coming to church and seemed genuinely touched by the message, although they had not yet committed their lives to Christ.

"We want you to come to our house, Albert," they pressed. "The next time you visit our island, be sure and come to see us."

About ten days later he paddled over to the island they lived on. Usually he used his outboard motor on his canoe, but with gas $1.50 a gallon and his pocketbook more slender than usual, he paddled.

After making a couple of other stops it was almost midnight when he finally got to Emile's. In a land where the sun doesn't go to bed until eleven o'clock in the summertime a call at midnight was not out of the ordinary. But Albert was very tired.

"Do you want to sing?" he asked them, fumbling in the Bible bag for the song books.

"Yes." Smiles lighted their dark faces.

"We'll sing two songs, O.K.?"

He was thinking about the long trip home.

When they finished singing he read a portion from the Bible. Emile pulled their mattress and blankets from the wall.

"We'll kneel on this to pray, Albert."

They knelt and began to pray. Albert hadn't quite realized how sleepy he was until he got on his knees. After a few sentences his voice trailed off. For five or six minutes all was silent. Suddenly his head jerked up and consciousness came slowly back. He became aware of where he was and, opening his eyes, he glanced to his right. Emile and Rose were still kneeling, waiting patiently for him to continue.

"Dear God," he went on, embarrassment flushing his thin

cheeks, "bless this home and make Yourself real to the people who live here. . . . ."

Since then Albert has been able to lead them both to Christ.

*   *   *

Barney died at Island Lake just before New Year's. He was a young man, a Christian, and highly respected in the community. As was their custom, the family and friends made plans to spend two nights with the body before it was buried. People would come and leave, but there would always be somebody present. Before the wake was over practically every one in the settlement would spend some time in the room where the body was kept. At regular intervals there would be singing and speaking.

It was decided that the night watch for Barney would be held in the council house and that he would be buried near the Bible school.

"We would like to have you speak, Albert," the father said.

When the slender Saulteaux reached the council house shortly before nine o'clock the building was filled with people. A few minutes later he got to his feet.

"There is a big tree on Savage Island, along the shore," he began. "The roots are dug right into the rocks. The tree stands firm and no wind can blow it over. It is a very strong tree."

"Hmmmm," a fat Indian man fifty years old or so murmured. He knew the tree Albert was talking about. Many times he had marvelled at it.

"Barney's life was like that tree. His faith was strong. It is like the Bible says. He is like a tree growing by the water. He bears fruit and his leaves don't get brown or die . . .

"The trees that grow in the bush are weak. They haven't put down good roots. And when the wind comes they go down easy.

"Jesus makes good strong roots for our lives—He gives us the only roots that hold. If you will confess your sin and put your trust in Him, He will hold you true."

Joe, the fat one, was looking up into Albert's eyes, clinging to each word.

"Maybe you have already decided for Christ," the speaker went on. "If you have, God wants you to stand firm and to live a good Christian life. He wants you to read the Bible and pray and witness for Him.

"Or, maybe you would like to be a Christian but you are afraid you will be tempted or have trouble at home if you do. . . . Think about that tree over on Savage Island. That tree has to fight against the wind. The waves pound at its feet and the ice piles up against it in the spring. But that tree stands firm.

"Christians who are tempted or have people make fun of them or persecute them grow strong like that tree. The Christian who has everything easy doesn't put down good roots. A big temptation comes and 'poof.' Down he goes!"

As far as Joe was concerned there was only him and Albert in the council house. Every word the youthful pastor spoke was for him alone.

The speaker finished and some of the visitors left, but Joe stayed on, quiet and thoughtful.

At midnight they opened the coffin, as was their custom. Albert spoke again.

He went home at four in the morning, but Joe remained until six, scarcely changing his position.

*   *   *

Rhoda was putting porridge on the table for a late breakfast when they heard a tractor going across the lake.

"They're going to cut wood, I guess," Albert said, shivering. "It's going to be cold out there for those fellows."

That evening a friend stopped by Albert's house with the news. "Did you know that Joe drowned today?"

"Joe?" Albert couldn't remember him at first.

"The fat one. You know. He was at Barney's wake last night."

"What happened?"

"They went to cut wood, and on the way home they went through the ice. Bill got out, but Joe couldn't swim and he was too big for Bill to hold up. His hands slipped." He gestured Bill's helplessness. "Joe was gone."

Nausea swept over Albert. Only the night before he had preached to Joe. And Joe had been visibly stirred. Now he was gone. There would never be another chance of reaching him for Christ.

Albert sat with some of the Christians in the settlement that evening.

"I didn't really give him the gospel hard enough last night," he told them miserably. He sat there crying to know, but I didn't give it to him strong enough. . . Maybe he would have become a Christian and be in Heaven now if I had spoken the way I should have!"

*   *   *

Albert Tait is only one of the growing number of Indian workers who are carrying such a large portion of the work of the Northern

Canada Evangelical Mission. They have a burden for their people and a firm desire to present Christ to them.

Billy Jackson is one of those evangelists. Billy was teaching at the Lac La Biche Indian Bible School the winter Barney Lacendre was there.

"The other teachers were good," Barney said with characteristic bluntness. "They knew our language and could explain the Bible real good, but oh, that Billy Jackson! Whenever I had something that I didn't understand I could go to Billy and he could explain it to me."

Home base for Bill is Little Buffalo, a village in the Peace River area of Northern Alberta. The work is too new to have an organized church as yet and Bill is called upon to travel so much that he hasn't been able to devote the time to it that he would like, but the local people look on him as their pastor. Missionaries look on him as one of their more effective evangelists and he has done a great deal of work in Bible camps throughout the summer.

Stan Williams is carrying on the same type of ministry as Jackson, and so is Raymond Sparklingeyes. Williams is working among the four thousand Indians on Manitoulin Island. He has a church building and the services are quite well attended, but the men in the area are slow to take an interest. Much of his work is in small Bible studies in his home.

Raymond Sparklingeyes is working on his home reserve at Goodfish Lake, Alberta. It is slow, as all work among the Indians is slow, and frequently discouraging, but it continues. He, too, will be travelling to different villages having an evangelistic ministry along with his work on the reserve and in summer Bible camps.

Benjie Nattaway has long been the Indian pastor of the work at Gods River, Manitoba. Like most Indian congregations, his is unable to support him completely. For that reason he works part time for the local free trader clerking and interpreting.

Benjie has been unable to break the stern resolve of the local men against the gospel, but there are a number of Christian women and young people. With his help the young people built the church they use at Gods River.

"The native evangelists face problems and difficulties we know nothing about," Ray Bradford said. "They have to have our deep interest and our prayer support if they are going to be effective witnesses for God."

Chapter 21

The problems of growth.

The directors of the Indian Bible Camp on Jeannette Lake north of Meadow Lake were desperate. The date for their annual Indian Bible camp was approaching, they had a capacity registration, and an acute shortage of counsellors.

"We're in for trouble unless we can get some help somewhere, and fast."

Then someone remembered the newly instituted summer workers' program. A frantic telephone call brought five or six young Bible school student men to help.

"They actually saved our camp for us," Abe Heppner said.

A hundred kids from Buffalo Narrows poured into the camp. Someone had started the rumor among them that this was going to be the most wonderful camp they had ever attended. There would be free airplane rides, free speed boat rides, all the water skiing they wanted, and no chapel. They weren't very happy when they found that they were wrong on all counts.

The young volunteer workers, some the sons of veteran missionaries, stepped into the situation forcefully. They imposed discipline, but with a considerate hand. Their own bubbling good nature was soon reflected in their youthful charges. Because of them the camp was effective.

1970 was the first year for the summer workers' program. The mission board had been watching the efforts of other missions along these lines with increasing interest. They not only needed the work done that a group of dedicated young Bible school and college students could do, but they felt that by exposing summer workers to the needs of the northern Indians there might be a possibility of bringing some of them into the North.

We weren't thinking only of our own mission in this," Bradford explained. "We wanted to challenge them for God and the northern Indian people. We feel that our program will have been a success if young men and women are brought north to work whether they associate themselves with us or not."

Recruiting for the summer program, now officially known as Northern Missionary Training Camp, is done by the deputation secretary as he visits Bible schools. The requirements are simple. They want students who have completed one or two years of Bible school or college so they are solidly established spiritually, and are old enough to be given responsibility.

The screening given summer candidates is not as intensive as that for full-time missionaries, but an effort is made to find out something about the applicants. A short application has been developed and references are required to screen out those who might be looking for adventure or are trying to run away from personal problems.

The summer work begins with a week of orientation by veteran missionaries. They are taught something of the technique of missionary work, and as much as possible about the culture of the people with whom they will be working. They are taught how to cope with spirit manifestations, should they encounter it, and a certain amount of teaching on the victorious Christian life.

At the end of orientation they are sent out, two to a team, with a senior missionary as supervisor. It is his responsibility to keep in contact with them, visiting their villages from time to time should they be in that type of ministry, and counselling them. The guidance for those in camp work is somewhat different in that they are constantly with older missionaries. Yet the purpose is the same.

At the end of six weeks of actual service for the Lord the summer workers are brought back to the base camp. There they will share the testimonies as to what the Lord has done for them and what He has done out in the villages. They will also be able to share experiences and discuss the field problems they had to face.

The field diaries which each summer worker is required to keep are turned over to the director, Art Tarry, who heads up the Northern Missionary Training Camp.

"By going over the diaries," he said, "we can tell if there are any unusual personality or personal problems among the students.

The diaries may also pin-point difficulties in the field we would otherwise not know about."

Twenty-one young people participated in the program in 1970 and it is anticipated that there will be a much larger group in the years to come.

"The interest and results of our first year indicate that this is going to be an effective arm of the work," Ray Bradford concluded.

*   *   *

The camp work of the NCEM has always taken an important place in the thinking of the missionaries. There are nine camps now, from Alberta through northern Quebec.

Kids who won't go to Sunday school or listen to a gospel message or even read a tract will often go to camp. At camp they are away from the home situation for a week and the counsellors and speakers are able to spend enough time with them to make an impact.

At the Stoney Lake Camp near Big River several years ago practically every kid from one Indian village made decisions for Christ. Some fell away, to be sure. Some were ridiculed by their families and friends until they decided they could not live the way they should. But others stood firm and true. They have come back in later years and a number of them give evidence of marked spiritual growth.

Most of the camps are in English, although one or two still operate in Cree.

*   *   *

For a number of years the work of the NCEM was carried on in a semi-casual manner. There were few missionaries involved and when they had a matter to work out the Board could make decisions from personal knowledge of the situation. But as the Lord blessed and the work grew the work became more complex. Several major problems faced the administration.

The first was that of location. Meadow Lake had been the location of headquarters simply because that was where the first organizational meetings were held. Later it proved impractical. There was no dependable public transportation, for one thing. They were not serviced by an airline and rail transportation and postal service were not good.

If the headquarters was to remain at Meadow Lake it would involve a good deal of money to bring the buildings up to standard.

Prince Albert had all the qualifications for a headquarters' location. That city was on an airline route and had good rail and postal service. There was an excellent highway, and it was just as close to the NCEM workers as was Meadow Lake. Moreover there was a building available, a former Catholic boarding school. The Board made an offer for the building, one much lower than its actual value, but feeling that if the move was of God He would provide the building. The offer was accepted and the move initiated.

Only the Mission Press operated by Owen Salway and Abe Heppner remained in Meadow Lake.

But more changes were to come—changes that were much more important in the terms of the effectiveness and total impact of the mission.

Previously the Board of Directors had handled most of the administrative work. An Executive Committee was set up within the Board to handle certain responsibilities. Missionaries who had lived far from Meadow Lake had long felt that they were being neglected simply because of the long distances involved. In order to do a better job at the local level two field councils were set up, one in the east and one in the west. Those councils were close enough to be of real service to the local missionaries. The change has made a more closely knit, effective organization.

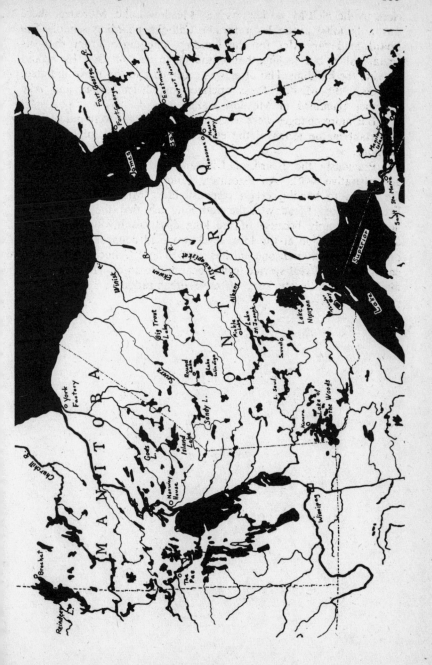

Chapter 22

The Windigo will walk again.

The time came when the Matthews family was to move to Round Lake. They all looked forward to it eagerly. They had enjoyed their time at Pickle Lake, and it had been rewarding, especially among the young people. But they had long been hearing about Round Lake and longed to go there. They wondered if the revival fires were still burning after so many years.

The children went up to the new station a few days ahead of their parents and an Indian couple came over to stay with them. The girls had great fun fixing meals for them.

"And tonight," they announced, "we're going to have blueberries."

The Indian woman eyed the bowl of berries before her and then looked up at her husband shyly. She didn't know how to use a spoon, they realized moments later. He nodded at her. She picked up the bowl with one hand and began to eat the berries as one would eat an ice cream cone. When she finished she wiped the inside of the bowl with her finger and carefully licked it off.

Buzz and Evelyn Matthews soon discovered that the revival at Round Lake, although subdued by the years, was still a vital force in the lives of the people. They could feel it before anyone spoke to them about things of the Lord. It was evident in the way they came to greet the new missionaries; in the way they helped to move the Matthews' personal belongings into the house.

Buzz soon found that the customs that had been established

when McComb was there were still strong within them. If a spiritual problem troubled someone he would come for help with it, whether it was morning, evening or in the middle of the night. They came continually, seeking answers to their questions, eagerly seeking to know more of the things of God.

"They can wake me up at any time," Buzz said, excited by the fact that they were actually with a people who longed to hear more of Christ. "I've never seen people, either Indian or white, who have such a hunger for God. They want to understand the Scriptures, know the will of the Lord, and have someone pray with them."

"It thrilled us both," his wife said later. "In fact it thrilled our entire family."

After the Matthews family was transferred to Round Lake it was decided that telephones should be put in there. In order to do this a diesel generating plant had to be installed and the missionary's home was supplied with electricity. Then, some months later something went wrong with the engine during the night. Almost before anyone was up the next morning word had *spread that Windigo (the Evil Spirit) had shut off the plant.

The children were frightened at school and an indefinable uneasiness seemed to settle over the village. There was no laughter or loitering on the paths.

There was a different sort of problem at the Matthews home. There was to be an elders' prayer meeting there that evening and the children were faced with the problem of playing outside or going to visit at the home of a friend for an hour or so. Possibly because nobody else was outside that evening Chuck went to the pastor's house next door. They had a son about the same age.

Old Grandma was sitting in the living room, her crutch and cane not far from her trembling hands. Her gaze darted fearfully about the room.

"The Windigo is going to walk again tonight," she said in her pinched, sing-song voice. "It is the time of the full moon. He is going to walk again tonight."

The boys sat down across from her.

"How do you know he's going to walk?" her grandson asked.

Her voice lowered as though she feared the evil spirit would hear her. "I saw the eyes of the wolf out in the bush."

"There's no wolf out there," Chuck said skeptically. "What do you mean, you saw the eyes of the wolf?"

But she was not dissuaded. "There's Windigo. Really! I saw his eyes out in the bush. I know he's going to walk again tonight!"

---

* 'By moccasin telegraph,' Mrs. Matthews relates, referring to the phenomenon mentioned earlier.

"We have the power of Christ," the missionary's son told her. "We don't have to be afraid."

Her sunken eyes grew wide with fear and her hands trembled.

"Don't talk that way!" she warned him. "Don't talk that way! If you go out you will die tonight!" She leaned forward. "The Windigo is mad. And he will come! You'd better be careful!"

By this time the entire family was listening to her. Fear surged through them like an electric charge.

"I'll go outside and nothing will hurt me," Chuck continued. "I don't need to be afraid when I have the power of the Spirit. You should come outside and prove to yourself that the Lord is able to take care of you . . . ."

As he continued to talk to her she began to quiet. And at last she seemed to gain courage.

"I will do this," she said. "I will go out and see if the power of the Lord is able to take care of me." There was a long pause. "If someone will go with me."

Chuck Matthews went outside, stayed for a time, and came back.

"See, nothing happened to me," he told her. "You don't need to be afraid."

She looked about, her dark face troubled.

"I *want* to go out," she said hesitantly.

Her young granddaughter came over to her.

"I'll go with you, Grandma."

The old lady's face lighted briefly. She managed a thin smile at the girl and struggled to her feet. Together they approached the door. Once at the door, however, their courage weakened. They stopped for a moment. The sun was just going down and the long twilight of summer was almost as bright as midday. But that did not seem to matter, so great was their fear of Windigo. They both turned, fearfully, towards Chuck.

"Nothing is going to hurt you," he assured them.

The little girl's hand went out, turned the door knob, and they moved, mechanically, out into the yard. They went forward a few steps, stopped, and went forward again.

Chuck watched, praying for them silently. Only a lad, himself, he had been living among the Indians for an important period of his young life, knew them and their ways, and was deeply concerned about seeing them throw off their pagan superstitions and put their whole trust in Christ.

Then, without warning, it happened.

"I can't do it, Grandma!" the girl screamed. Leaving the frightened old woman, she turned and fled, sobbing, into the house.

Grandma leaned heavily on her cane and crutch. So great was her terror she seemed unable to move.

"Somebody come and get me," she cried. "Please! Somebody come and get me!" A low, tremoring moan escaped her lips. Fear had stolen reason. She was crying now and muttering to herself—half words—half formless sounds of terror. "Please come and help me in!"

"I'll come, Grandma!" another girl called out.

She started bravely enough, but after a few steps her love for her grandmother was overpowered by her dread of the unseen Windigo. As she hesitated, turned and fled towards the house, the lad who was Chuck's age crowded past her.

"Don't worry, Grandma! I'll come and get you."

He reached the trembling woman who, by this time was unable to speak.

"There now! Let me help you get turned around and—and—" His voice died in his throat. It had been one thing to stand beside Chuck in the house and to draw strength from his calm assurance and faith in Christ. It was quite another to be out in the yard with his grandmother who was so terrified she could scarcely move. She took a step or two, leaning most of her weight heavily on him.

"Hurry, Grandma!"

His efforts to get her to hurry so flustered her that her entire being began to tremble and she could scarcely move.

"W-Windigo," she muttered almost incoherently. "W-W-Windigo w-w-walks to——"

That was too much for the Indian boy. He broke away from her and dashed for the house.

"Don't leave me!" Her voice crescendoed plaintively. "Don't leave me!"

With that Chuck went out to her.

"Come on, Grandma," he said calmly. "I'll help you."

She was still sobbing in near hysteria as he led her into the house and got her seated once more.

She was still mumbling and crying softly. The other members of the household stood silently about, faces somber, eyes dark with fear. Although no one except Grandma was still crying, the tension seemed to build. The pastor's wife had stopped doing the dishes and was sitting in a straight-backed chair staring from one to the other in silence.

Chuck tried to talk to them, but they answered in monosyllables, if at all. Endlessly, the minutes dragged by.

The house was so hushed with fear the sudden rattling at the door was like the exploding of a rifle.

Breathing stopped! Heads jerked up! Eyes snapped around to stare at the cabin door!

"W-w-what was that?" the boy asked fearfully.

"Windigo!" Grandma cried. Horror rushed to her voice. "I knew he was going to walk tonight. I knew he was going to walk tonight! . . ." She began to moan and rock back and forth in her kitchen chair. "What is going to become of us? What will happen to us all?"

"I'll see what it is," Chuck said, getting to his feet and starting for the door. "It probably isn't anything that—"

"*Don't!*" the pastor's wife shrieked in terror. Never before had anyone ever heard her utter a single word of English. "Don't!"

With that all of them rushed to the bedroom. All, that is, except Grandma. She sat there, transfixed by fear, moaning and groaning in a queer, sing-song wail.

"If you don't want me to open the door," Chuck said, "I won't. But I just thought I'd see what it is that's out there."

Once they saw that he wasn't going to open the door and risk letting the dread Windigo in to get them they began to drift back from the bedroom.

It was half an hour later or more before the pastor's wife would let Chuck open the door.

"Look," he said. "It's only my dog. I guess you knew I was over here, didn't you, fella."

Once the fear began to lessen, Chuck turned to his Indian pal to try and talk with him about the spiritism they were letting blight their lives.

"You're a believer," he began, "and your father is the pastor here. How does he feel about all of this."

There was a brief hesitation.

"He isn't sure," the boy's mother answered in Cree. "He doesn't know what to think."

It was nearly dark when the pastor came home. He left the Matthews house rapidly, looking back over his shoulder as though afraid the Windigo was going to sweep out of the bush and carry him off. The farther he got from the missionary's house the faster he walked until by the time he reached home he was almost running.

Several days later Buzz talked with his son, Chuck, about the events that had taken place that night.

"I think you were able to help them a little, Chuck," he said. "I was over there this morning and they were talking about it.

They don't seem to be quite so much afraid as they were before. They saw that you aren't afraid of Windigo and nothing happened."

"I can't understand why they're like that, Dad," the boy replied. "They're Christian. They read in the Bible the way God promises to take care of them. Why can't they realize there's nothing to that crazy stuff?"

"It looks crazy to us," Buzz answered. "And, I guess it is crazy to be afraid of a thing like 'the Windigo.' But we've got to realize that these people have been brought up on superstitution and fear. Their people have believed this sort of thing for hundreds of years. Even though they do accept Christ as their Saviour and put their trust in Him they find it difficult to make a clean break with these things in their lives."

*   *   *

It was midwinter at Round Lake. The mercury stood near the bottom of the thermometer. The ice had long since silenced the restless water and the snow was deep on the trails. Only those who had to be there ventured to cross the lake.

From the warmth of their home Evelyn Matthews saw a small, dark figure out on the lake, struggling with a toboggan. For a moment or two she watched.

"Buzz, come here."

He joined her at the window.

"Whoever that is sure has a heavy load," he said. "He ought to have dogs to pull a toboggan like that."

Her lips pursed.

"It looks like a woman to me."

"It can't be."

By this time the person pulling the toboggan had reached shore and was at the foot of the hill.

"It is a woman!" Buzz exclaimed.

Wriggling into his parka and boots he hurried out to see the thin, work wasted wife of one of the commercial fishermen pulling a toboggan load of fish.

"Here," he said. "Let me help you with this."

Amazement gleamed for an instant in her fatigue-dulled eyes. This was something that had never happened to her before. Then shyness overcame her surprise.

"Oh no," she protested. "I can manage."

She tried, feebly, to start the toboggan to moving again. In her culture it was unthinkable that a man would help her, and especially a white man. Buzz knew all of that. But he knew the marks of exhaustion, too. He read the bone-weariness in her slow, uncertain movements and the pallor that had crept over her dark face.

"I'll take it up the hill for you."

Even with his strength it was difficult to get the load up the little rise. She did not thank him, but there was silent gratitude in her eyes.

"She never would have managed it without help," he told his wife later.

They already knew much about the woman we will call Sarah. They had a large family, and her husband's income from trapping and commercial fishing was small and uncertain. It was difficult for them to have food on the table at all, and there were times when the entire family went hungry. They owned few dishes and no cups or glasses, drinking their tea or water from cans.

"You have to understand something of Indian ways to understand the problems of this poor woman," Mrs. Matthews said. "By culture her husband, even though he was a Christian, would not help her with what he considered was woman's work. By culture, her children like all the other Indian youngsters were not taught to mind or to help at home. She had to do everything herself.

"She gathered wood from the bush, tried desperately to keep her big brood clothed, and washed all of their clothing by hand. She was one who appreciated cleanliness. I've seen her on her hands and knees pushing a rag across the floor to sweep because she didn't have a broom."

The death of a son the year before put a blight on her life. The illness of her youngest baby that had taken the little one to a hospital outside where she had been for the past six months knotted the poor woman's stomach and kept her from sleeping nights.

It was small wonder a few months after the incident with the toboggan that Buzz and Evelyn Matthews were called to her home one night.

"What is wrong with her?" the missionary asked her stepson.

"She is sick in her heart." Discouragement at last had overwhelmed her. She wanted to die and go to Heaven. She didn't want to live any more.

Her hands were icy cold and she was hysterical.

Quietly the missionary talked to her about the Lord and the strength He can give to face any problem. The Indian leaders of the church congregated around the bed, her husband with them, and prayed for her.

After a time she opened her eyes, turned to look at Evelyn Matthews and smiled gently.

"That smile meant more to me than anything that had happened to me, personally, since we came to the field," Evelyn said. "To think that with all the Indian women in the room, she would single me out. I could have cried!"

She became quiet as Buzz talked with her of the love of Christ and finally went to sleep and got a good night's rest. She was still in bed when the missionaries went over the next morning to see her.

Evelyn went to the kitchen for something to fix the ill woman to eat.

"Buzz," she called a moment later. "Look!" She swung open the cupboard doors. "There's nothing to eat in here. Not a single thing!"

He went to the Hudson's Bay Store for some soup.

There were huge sores on her legs and her strength was all but gone. It took weeks before her body could be built back to the place where her sores would heal. But at last she was well and able to do her own work again.

Sarah and her husband and children had not been coming to church, but after this experience they all began to attend regularly. Her life was still no easier than it had been before. She still had to work as hard. Neither her husband nor their children helped her. And yet there was a difference. She was trusting in her Lord for strength and courage. Though her way was hard she was able to sing and rejoice in Him.

Chapter 23

A journey completed.

It had been a long, cold winter at Round Lake. A great weariness settled over the people as the snow lingered. The skies were often dark and brooding and the sharp wind wore a bitter cutting edge. Then the clouds scattered and the spring sun once more began to smile. The drifts disappeared and the winter ice started to rot.

The break-up was not far behind. And when it came, in May, piling great jagged chunks high on the beaches, it was as though the heart suddenly found its song again. Commercial fishermen were repairing their boats and getting their outboard motors tuned against the soon-coming day when the lake would be free of ice. Children, who found enjoyment in the snow, were now revelling in the gentle kiss of the warming breeze and trying to forget that they should be studying for the final exams they would soon be called upon to write.

Normally, Buzz Matthews was so busy he seldom took time off from his missionary duties. On this occasion he probably wouldn't even have thought about going out on the lake to fish had it not been for Lloyd Potts. For the past several days the Christian public school teacher had watched the ice disappear and talked about going fishing.

"The ice is almost gone, Buzz," he said. "And as soon as it is, you and I are going out to get some of those pickerel that should be biting."

"I haven't been fishing for a long time."

"And you ought to be ashamed of yourself. You've got a little break coming." He glanced at Mrs. Matthews. "And I think you ought to go along, too, Evelyn."

"Me?"

"That's right. You're like Buzz. You've been working too hard. The three of us are going fishing right after school one of these first nights."

The afternoon they chose could not have been worse for Evelyn. She hadn't finished her washing. The next day was the birthday of one of their daughters and she wasn't completely ready for that. There were two meetings coming up that needed a little attention, and she had a weekly half hour class of religious instruction in the school to prepare.

"I don't see how I can go tonight, Buzz," she said.

Chuck, who was looking forward to his fifteenth birthday in two weeks, waited until he was sure her answer was final.

"Mum," he said, "if you're not going, could I go?"

So the three of them went down to the canoe. The man who had come to fix the diesel engine on the generator started with them, but had them bring him back after they had gone a few hundred yards.

"It's too late for me," he said. "I'm going to be late enough getting home as it is."

It had been very warm all day and towards evening the wind came up.

"Will Daddy and Chuck be in for supper?" one of the girls asked.

Evelyn looked out at the waves.

"I imagine they'll have to wait until the wind goes down. We'll fix them something when they get in."

Shortly after dark the wind slacked off and Mrs. Matthews looked towards the lake again.

'If it stayed like this,' she thought silently, 'they ought to be home soon.'

But the lull only lasted for a few short minutes.

Without warning the storm hit. In one savage blast the hurricane-force whipped the still-rolling lake to a frenzy. Swells peaked, only to have the wind blow off the tops in ugly white froth and whip spray across the surface. They crashed into the beach with a deafening roar.

The *phone rang.

"We were wondering about Buzz," an Indian voice said. "Did they get in all right?"

---

* They had phones at Round Lake because a telephone company wanted to test the practicability of a combination radio-wire phone service (and the financial returns possible) into isolated communities.

"No, they aren't back yet."

"Did they take blankets?"

"No."

"Food?"

"No, but I'm really not too concerned about them. I'm sure they saw the storm coming and decided to wait it out. Don't worry about them. They'll surely be in tomorrow morning."

But the confidence Mrs. Matthews had as she talked on the phone melted as she sat alone at the window, staring out into the blackness of the night. The lake was whipped to an angry froth and the roar of the breakers crashing against the beach was undiminished all through the night.

At last weariness overtook the distraught missionary wife. She went into her bedroom and knelt to pray, committing her husband, her son and their companion to God. Presently she drifted off to sleep, but it was light and restless. Most of the night she listened for the sound of an engine that did not come.

Towards morning the wind finally began to go down.

At dawn Mrs. Matthews got up with great heaviness in her heart, and dressed. The school principal, also a Christian, was already up and standing on the shore, looking out across the big lake. His very presence there spoke of his own uneasiness.

He saw that Mrs. Matthews was up and came to the door.

"Don't you think we ought to organize a search party?" he asked. She noted the time.

"The wind hasn't been down very long," she said. "Perhaps we ought to give them a little time to get in before we do that."

"I'm going down and see Peter," he said, trying to hide his concern. "He's got a good canoe and the fastest motor on the lake."

In a few minutes he was back.

"Peter agrees with you, Evelyn. He thinks we ought to wait until seven o'clock before we start looking for them. He said Buzz's motor is small and they'll have to have a little time to get back."

Evelyn Matthews baked the birthday cake for her daughter, got breakfast for the children, and tried not to think about the thing that was gradually crowding all else out of her mind.

She and the school principal were not the only ones who were concerned about the missing fishermen. At seven o'clock that morning a number of boats went out to look for them. But it wasn't long until they were back.

"We checked some cabins down by the river," the spokesman said. "We thought they might be there. But there was no sign of them."

The ice in her heart began to grow.

"What do you think we ought to do now?" she asked.

"We'll have to get out a big search party."

'They're probably on the shore of an island somewhere,' she told herself, trying to ignore the fear that was gnawing at the corners of her heart. Aloud she said, "Would it be all right for me to go along?"

"You can go in my canoe," the interpreter for the church said.

She got the girls off to school and left their two year old baby in the care of the principal.

They started having school that morning, but some time before noon they dismissed classes for the day. The teachers couldn't keep their minds on the lessons and the students, even though they lacked the experience to fully understand, were disturbed by what had happened. The Indians were gathering in homes all over the village.

The search was carefully organized and skilfully conducted. Each boat was assigned a certain area and given the responsibility for covering it.

The search was bleak and unrewarding for the canoe Mrs. Matthews was in. The empty stretches of beach, the rocky points seemed to mock at her. The men in the canoe were concerned about her and very kind, but there was nothing anyone could say or do to help. Nothing except finding the missing fishermen alive and well.

It was nearly noon and they were still out on the lake when they saw a canoe racing towards them, its occupants waving.

"They've found something," the interpreter murmured in English.

As the canoe glided to a stop beside them the men began to talk very rapidly in Cree.

"What is it?" Evelyn broke in impatiently. "What did they find?"

At first the interpreter continued to talk to the Indians without replying to her. Then he turned slowly. His voice was tender.

"They have found the canoe out in the lake," he said, "it was tipped over." He went on to talk about the motor, gesturing with his arm.

They went over to the canoe as fast as possible. It had been found drifting in the middle of the lake, far west of where it should have been, and about a mile from shore. It was filled with water. Only the tip of the bow was showing.

"As we got near shore," Mrs. Matthews said, "I began to realize that the interpreter was trying to tell me that the motor was on full throttle."

That meant they had been out in the lake when the sudden storm hit! There was no hope they would be found!

The shore of the settlement was alive with color as the canoe that held Mrs. Matthews drew near. All the Indians in the village were down to see her.

"As I saw them," she said, "it was as though I was standing at a distance looking at myself. My only thought was, 'Lord, give me strength to show these people the love of the Lord Jesus in the face of something like this!' "

Mrs. Matthews looked at the people waiting for her on shore and bowed her head again. It wasn't the normal thing as far as she, personally, was concerned, to be thinking of them at a time like this, she realized. She was as weak, as given to emotion as anyone. In her own strength she could do nothing.

Life didn't even seem worth living.

But as she prayed she grew increasingly aware that Christ was already working in her heart.

As soon as she reached shore the women crowded close about her. They threw their arms around her and sobbed, trembling in their grief.

Sally, whose husband had drowned in the lake some years before, could find no words. She clung to Evelyn Matthews in agony.

"We have a great God," the missionary managed. "He will help us."

There, near the steps of the house stood her oldest daughter, her tiny young face gray with shock and grief. Evelyn longed to break from the people and rush to her daughter. But she could not risk hurting them now in their time of sorrow.

After the women had expressed their sympathy the men came, one by one. They extended their hands, tears flowing down their dark, weather-beaten cheeks. Tears in the eyes of men who probably hadn't cried since they were children.

At last the young widow was able to get into the house to her daughter's side. The people followed, not knowing what they could do, but reluctant to leave.

"Have they told you?" she asked her ashen daughter.

"Yes," she answered simply.

The other children were still with the school principal.

"I wanted to go to them," Mrs. Matthews related some time afterwards, "but I knew I had to be with our people for a time."

The old Grandma who had been so afraid of the Windigo seemed almost out of her mind with grief. Words failed her and she was sobbing so bitterly she could scarcely stand.

"Could you please give her your chair?" Evelyn asked one of those who was sitting down.

*   *   *

Even in times of tragedy there were things that had to be done. Evelyn Matthews called Stan Collie at The Pas, Manitoba and he and his wife flew over immediately. Then she notified the telephone company because Buzz had been taking care of their office for them, and gave the police officer all the details she knew of the accident.

The mountie went away shaking his head.

"The people must have thought a lot of your husband," he told her.

"They did."

"And you're taking this very well. Very well, indeed."

'I can do all things through Christ which strengtheneth me,' she told herself.

"We'll bring in equipment and start dragging for the bodies as soon as possible," he said.

But the Indians didn't wait for the authorities. They improvised their own dragging equipment and set to work. They were out day after day dragging the big lake unless the wind was too high for them to be on the lake.

Evelyn decided that when they were found she wanted their bodies buried at Round Lake and asked the people to make caskets for them.

"We couldn't do it good enough," one of them protested.

But she assured them it was just what Buzz and Chuck would have wanted.

Stan Collie went with her to the Indian cemetery. The only spot large enough for both graves together, except for a rocky place at the back, was almost exactly in the center.

"That would be a beautiful symbol of Buzz's life," she said, "right in the center of the people he loved so much. But he's white. I don't know how they would feel about him and Chuck being buried there. I wouldn't want to pick that location on my own."

That evening she had a caller. The chief had come to see them on other occasions, but this was different. He was straight as a spruce tree—almost regal.

"Our people loved your husband," he said. "We consider it a great privilege to have him and your son buried in the center of our cemetery."

The bodies were not found for some time and the people crowded around Evelyn Matthews in an effort to help.

"People are calling me," the interpreter said, "wanting to know if they can do something for you."

Mrs. Collie was there with her, but there was very little that needed doing. The Indian women made the beds, swept, chopped the wood and carried water.

Even that was not enough. One woman cut up one of her own dresses and made the widowed missionary a skirt. Another gave her a skirt of new material that was much too big for her. Very obviously the woman had made it for herself.

"The skirts certainly weren't what I would have chosen, but I wore them just the same. I had to let them know how deeply I appreciated their gifts."

Another woman came and pressed a dollar bill into her hand. There had been sickness in her family and they hadn't been able to hunt and trap the way they usually did. Money they sorely needed themselves was brought to the missionary out of love.

One little girl who had nothing else to give wrapped a torn, faded bandana and gave it to her. These gifts were not from the affluent, but the poor. People who had very little, and any gift was a sacrifice.

But the gift that touched her heart the most was that which was given to her by Grandma who lived next door.

Grandma's eyes had been failing her until she couldn't read the Scriptures. She would come over and ask Buzz Matthews to read to her. Often, after such a session he would take a magic marker pencil and print out a Bible verse in large letters on a sheet of paper. Proudly she would take it home and hang it up so she could look at it and read it.

It was through Grandma that Chuck learned the Cree he knew. She was in the Matthews home often. And, each time, just before she left, she would take out a small travel clock and have Buzz set it by his pocket watch, although it kept very good time.

Now she called Evelyn to her side on the sofa.

"I want you to have this," she said. She handed her the little clock.

The white woman stared at it. It was easily Grandma's most prized possession. This couldn't be right. She was misunderstanding the old woman. She called the interpreter and he came over.

"Yes," he said, after talking with Grandma. "She wants to give it to you. She said that your son was very dear to her because he would come over to her house and talk to her and try to learn her language. And she said she loved your husband as her own son."

The little travel clock became one of Evelyn Matthews' most prized possessions.

*   *   *

Following a visit and rest back home in the States Mrs. Matthews and her daughters returned to their beloved Indians. Despite the fact that the Indians at Round Lake loved her so much and her husband and son are buried there, it seemed advisable to send her to the Bible school at Island Lake where life wouldn't be quite so rigorous.

The decision to go North was one that pleased the girls.

"I want to be a missionary just like you and daddy when I get big," the oldest girl confided.

After two years or so at Island Lake Mrs. Matthews felt it wise to go back to the States where she could put her children in school for the higher grades. She has since remarried.

*   *   *

The North is harsh and relentless and demanding of everyone who would live there. But there is a glory in the North among God's people, and especially among His servants there. Gradually souls are being won for Christ and closed hearts are being stormed with the gospel.

When the battle is won it will be because of men like Buzz Matthews—yes and his wife, Evelyn—and the many other missionaries who have journeyed to a lonely land to live under difficult circumstances that the people might be reached for the Lord Jesus Christ.